On Our Way

Travels in Europe and Ireland

Hugh Oram

 www.trafford.com
North America & international
toll-free: 1 888 232 4444 (USA & Canada)
fax: 812 355 4082

Dedication

To my wonderful and much loved wife, Bernadette, always a perfect companion along life's way and during all our travels together

Acknowledgements

During all our travels together, Bernadette has been an incredible companion, well able to cope with the vicissitudes of travelling, brilliant at finding logistical solutions and always a most delightful and charming person to accompany me on all my travels, her companionship leavened with a great sense of intellectual curiosity and humour. I'd also like to thank Maria Gillen in Athlone for all her help and encouragement while I was writing this book. I'd also like to thank Aisling Curley in Dublin for all her practical support while I was writing the text and Dean Lochner of the Bondi Group in Dublin for all his technical assistance. I'd also like to thank the innumerable people along the way, who provided help, encouragement and sometimes inspiration, while we were on our travels. In many cases, lasting friendships were formed, a wonderful bonus to all our travels.

Travels in Europe

1958 France

This was my first trip abroad, to France, at the tender age of 15, and I managed all the complicated itineraries entirely my myself, including negotiating the journey across Paris from the Gard du Nord to the Gare de Lyon. It was quite a trek, my first journey outside England, leaving from Snow Hill station in Birmingham, travelling to London, then getting the boat train to Dover and then on from Calais to Paris, crossing Paris to the Gare de Lyon and travelling to Lyon, where I was met by the family I was staying with. I did it all without a word of French and even managed to navigate the old fashioned payphones in the Gare de Lyon. In those days, French payphones used jetons.

I ended up in a small village near Mâcon, in the heart of the wine producing country surrounding Lyon. The village itself was amazingly quiet, since there were few cars on the road;this was only 13 years after the end of the second world war and France was still far from recovery. The house I stayed in was very large, but sparsely furnished. I remember vividly that the family I stayed with was large, with about a dozen members seated around the dinner table at night, in traditional French style. None of them had any English and I had no French, so I had to set about learning French, which I did in double quick order, so that I didn't miss out on any of the delicacies being served for dinner. When I arrived home in England a month later, I was substantially fluent in French, much to my own surprise and that of my family and school friends.

The only trip we did outside the village was to Lyon itself, where I remember vividly the great cathedral of Notre Dame de Fouvrière, set on a hill high above the city, the funicular railway that leads to the cathedral, the confluence of two mighty rivers, the Saone and the Rhône and all the dreary quaysides beside the rivers. I didn't get to explore the substantial Roman origins of the city and in 1958, all I can remember of the city is how dull, dreary and run-down it looked, long before its renaissance, especially as undoubtedly the leading centre in France for haute cuisine.

That particular trip can be dated precisely, because it coincided with the most serious attack on General de Gaulle, the man who led the Free French during the second world war and eventually went on to become a remarkable president, intensely French in his thoughts, desires and ambitions. I remember vividly going to the village cinema one night;the main film has faded totally from my memory but I have very detailed recollections of the black and white newsreel showing the bullet ridden car de Gaulle had been riding in near Paris. The attack came at the height of the opposition by French settlers in Algeria to any attempted peace settlement, which came anyway in 1962, when de Gaulle got his way and Algeria was given independence. The eight year battle by the settlers was lost and after the peace deal was made, many of the French settlers in Algeria, the pieds noirs, made their way to France, with many of them settling in the south of France.

Shortly afterwards, I went on another exchange visit to France, this time to the village of Nontron, population 3,500, in the Dordogne, where I stayed in the enormous 16th century chateau. It's a vast place, with 16 bedrooms. Currently, it's up for sale, for a mere €3 million. One of the trips I did when I was there was going to see the prehistoric cave paintings at Lascaux; it was a rare sight, because not long after, the caves were closed to the public, because all the condensation from people' s breaths was destroying the paintings.

1960 Italy

My first trip to Italy came in 1960, my third exchange visit abroad. The family I stayed with in Rome was French;the head of the family was the French military attaché in Rome. The family was very generous in taking me for car drives to many of the sights around Rome, such as the wine town of Frascati, to the east of Rome, with its marvellous vistas of lakes and cypress trees. Perhaps the most interesting of the trips close to Rome was to what had been the centre of Etruscan civilisation, long before the Roman empire began. In Rome itself, I saw most of the ancient ruins and many of the city's great churches, so much so that one began to merge into another in my mind. The one that made the greatest impression on me was St John of Lateran. Other sights in and near Rome included the beaches at Ostia Antica and what remains of the Appian Way.

The most impressive building in Rome is of course St Peter's, so I had a good look round there and the adjoining galleries, as well as getting an invitation to the studios of Vatican Radio, with its distinctive call sign. It was the first time I had seen inside radio studios and it was fascinating.

The family also took me on a trip down south, spending a night in Naples, where I got my first glimpse of the infamous slums of Naples, saw the view across the bay to Vesuvius, explored the 17th century royal palace, from where the kingdom of Naples was ruled until Italian unification absorbed the kingdom in the 1860s. Also near Naples, we went to see the mighty ruins of the three Greek temples at Paestum, once part of an ancient Greek city and said to be the most perfectly preserved of their kind. On the way back to Rome, we stopped off at the monastery at Monte Cassino. In 1944, a ferocious battle had been wages on the mountain slopes around the monastery, as Allied forces battled the Nazis. The monastery itself was largely ruined in that battle and when we were there in 1958, the mountain slopes were still very desolate and restoration of the monastery had barely begun. These days of course, it has long since been returned to its original splendour.

The train travel to Rome had been spectacular, an overnight journey from Paris. As dawn was breaking the next morning and I sat having my breakfast in the dining car of the train, the sun was rising over the sea along the Italian Riviera and it was a most spectacular sight. But inside Italy, I made an equally memorable train journey, from the ultra modern Stazioni Termini in Rome to Florence, a four hour journey in those days, but nowadays, taking less than half that time. The station had been built in Mussolini's time, part of his quest to make the trains in Italy run on time. I had but a few hours in Florence, but it was captivating, seeing the great cathedral, the Uffizi Galleries, the statue of David and of course the Ponte Vecchio, the medieval bridge lined with ancient shops on both sides, and spanning the River Arno. Altogether, it was a most memorable trip, also laced with humour. Going up to Florence, the Italian family who shared the wooden-seated compartment with me, spread out an enormous lunch on the seat and plonked down a gigantic chamber pot for their children to use! Patrick, the son of the French diplomat, had a great sense of humour and I remember vividly on one occasion when we were going to explore yet another ancient ruin in Rome, we saw a very ambitious pile of dog turds at the entrance. Patrick remarked: "Voilá, le sentinel!" Altogether, though, that month spent in Rome, with side trips to Naples and Florence, was a wonderful introduction to Italian life and culture. I even became inspired afterwards to follow a teach yourself Italian course on BBC radio, so that for a time, I was reasonably fluent in what is a marvellous Romantic language. The trip also had medical moments;I developed an acute dose of sinusitis and the family I was staying with were very good about arranging for a nurse to come and see me. She came two nights running, each time plunging a syringe filled with penicillin into my buttocks;at the time, it all seemed quite drastic, but I was over the malady in a couple of days. The memories of Rome itself live on within me to this day.

It also produced a lasting antipathy to the Olympic Games. I went to one of the running competitions in the Olympic Stadium in Rome and found the whole experience utterly boring. Ever since then, I've been singularly unmoved by the Olympics. Rome was due to be in the competition to find a venue for the 2024 Olympics, but wisely, Italy has decided to drop out and spend the money on much- needed services at home.

1962 Derry

October, 1962, was the beginning of a whole new adventure, when I came to live in Ireland for the first time.

I'd already been to Dublin but what I'd discovered there was little preparation for what I found in Derry. I found Derry in those days to be a depressing and depressed place, rife with social discrimination. The middle classes and the aristos were all living high on the hog and inevitably, their sympathies were entirely Unionist. They had little understanding of how the other half lived, the disenfranchised Catholics and Nationalists who in fact formed the majority population in the city. They were excluded from many of their civil rights and no-one in authority seemed to care a damn. It's awful that it took so much tragedy and violence to ensure that those civil rights were granted eventually. I've been back to Derry several times in recent years and it's remarkable how much the city has changed for the better, now that all its citizens are treated with equal respect.

I remember vividly the dreariness of places like Shipquay Street and the Diamond in the centre of Derry, with the Guildhall towering over the place. Among the few places were a little light relief could be enjoyed were the city centre bars, including the Waterloo, and the bars along the Strand Road. Magee University College wasn't much better;it was still in the grip of its Presbyterian heritage and the fact that it offered courses from Trinity College, Dublin, didn't soften the harshness. I hated the place with a vengeance and found studying an absurd waste of time;I did the sensible thing and left when I was halfway through my course and went to live somewhere much more civilised, cultured and interesting, Dublin. Some of the places I lived in Derry were frightful, including one flat in Orchard Street where the walls were literally running water. I also remember vividly writing a poem about an unfortunate elderly woman who went into the nearby Woolworth's and dropped dead, a truly banal place for a life to end.

Yet there were moments of joy in Derry, like the screening in Magee's Great Hall of the magnificent George Morrison film Mise Éire, made from newsreels shot in the aftermath of 1916 and during the war of independence. Seeing the film was absolutely electrifying and the entire audience was caught up in an emotional high, seeing the attempts at shaking off the authoritarian outside rule by Britain in most of Ireland. I honestly believe that screening that film in Derry was one of the key triggers for the forming of the civil rights movement in the North of Ireland and it's astonishing that it's only in recent years, 50 years on, that people from all sections of the community in the North are getting the rights that they are due.

Another place I lived in Derry was in a delapidated cottage in Galliagh, off the main road to Buncrana. In those days, it was right in the middle of the countryside, a far cry from the built-up area it has become today.

Living and studying in Derry was in many ways a horrible experience, but I always believe that even from the worst adversity can come hope. But I wouldn't write off Derry in its entirety, as I made many wonderful friends there, some of whom I've kept in touch with to the present day.

1968 Prague

After I'd arrived in Derry in 1962 as an utterly useless third level student, it took about five or six years for me to start finding my feet. I spent some time back in Birmingham, which I hated, although at one stage, I enjoyed living in a caravan alongside a house that took in all Irish lodgers. I shared meals with them and it was an amazingly educative experience;they all had really tough life stories to tell and many were nostalgic for an Ireland they'd had to leave in order to survive economically, but they were a good humoured lot. I admired their spirit and their stories, quite apart from their love for Ireland, an affection improved by being so far away from what was then a very economically depressed country, especially the West of Ireland.

But after I'd managed to land a job with the then newly founded Business & Finance magazine, in Creation Arcade off Grafton Street, Dublin, I started to find my feet in the media business. It took a while to make the move from the commercial side, where I was no natural born salesperson, to editorial. That journey also encompassed my journey to Belfast, where I spent the end of the 1960s and which I didn't leave until 1974. It's ironic that while I was getting an excellent training in feature writing at the Belfast Newsletter that I met my future wife, Bernadette Quinn, one day in August, 1970, when I was in Dublin researching and writing a feature on mining exploration in Ireland, north and south.

However, a couple of years before I'd first met Bernadette, I was getting on well at Business & Finance. One of the contacts I made there was Miroslav Hudec, who was the Czechoslovak commercial attaché in Ireland. He and his family were most hospitable and on many occasions, I enjoyed their company and their generosity very much, at their home at Foxfield Park in Raheny, Dublin. The upshot of all that was that it was decided to do a supplement in Business & Finance on Irish-Czechoslovak business relations and I was given the go-ahead to go to Prague and get everything organised. With free air tickets there and back and a wonderful exchange rate on the black market in Prague for US dollars, the logistics of the trip worked out fine.

I ended up being given bed and breakfast accommodation in an apartment in Narodni, the main street right in the centre of Prague. I went round all the government agencies in Prague to get all the editorial and advertising copy organised and it was all done so efficiently that I had most of my time to myself. I saw all the sights of Prague, including the majestic cathedral and castle, the Mozart house and museum, the Charles Bridge, Wencelas Square, Tyn Square with its medieval clock, in fact most of the sights in and around Prague, long before it became such a popular western tourist destination. I was well aware that the so-called Prague Spring was under way, a very modest attempt to liberalise the country, but in practical terms, it made little difference, it was more hope of mild improvements rather than anything else. Service in places like banks and restaurants remained absolutely desperate. But it did rattle the Soviets, who saw this as a potential threat to their empire, and a couple of days after I'd returned to Dublin, the invasion by all the Soviet bloc countries, with the exception of Romania and Yugoslavia, was under way.

The invasion was world news, but of course, the western powers could do nothing to halt the invasion or ameliorate its worst effects. Somehow or other, I managed to get a visa to go back to Prague the following year, with a friend, I found it a very sullen place, with soldiers on almost every street corner. It took another 20 years before Czechoslovakia found its freedom, of sorts, with the country eventually divided into two separate countries.

1971 Amsterdam and Paris

This year, 1971, saw us taking another trip, this time to Amsterdam. At the time, I was writing a lot about the drinks trade and we got an invitation to visit the Advocaat factory there. These days, it can be hard to find the stuff, let alone hear any mention of it! Our host at Advocaat was very generous and I remember that he took us to an excellent lunch at the hotel where a short time before, Yoko Ono and her husband, John Lennon of the Beatles, had staged their love-in. We stayed in a small hotel in the centre of Amsterdam, a place that was noted for its minute loo. There was barely room to sit on the pot and that was that!On one memorable occasion, Bernadette got an urgent need to make the loo and rushed back through the city streets, recognised the street we were staying in by the clothes shop on the corner and with scarcely a second to spare, made the loo which had no room to spare!We saw many of the conventional sights in Amsterdam, including of course the ladies in the window. With all due respect, it was anything but erotic, the exact opposite in fact. In a subsequent trip not long after to Brussels, which must count as one of the most boring cities in Europe, we found exactly the same, a street where the women who were plying their wares were all sitting in windows. The only difference between Brussels and Amsterdam is that the women who were plying their wares in the former city had a sense of humour and gesticulated amusingly at Bernadette.

That year, 1971, also saw us making our first trip to Paris as a couple. We stayed in a small and spartan hotel, the Hotel

Taylor, in the rue Taylor in the 10th. It's a rather rundown part of Paris, but certainly very lively and I remember vividly going into a shoe shop on the adjacent boulevard St Martin and buying what were politely described as "brothel creepers". That year was the first in which we did a multitude of trips. In 1971, we also made a trip to London and to Plymouth, but while they were interesting, that particular excursion couldn't quite compete in the excitement stakes with Amsterdam.

1972 Peel, Isle of Man

This was the year when Bernadette Quinn and myself got married, in Peel in the Isle of Man. We'd met for the first time on August 13, 1970, when I went into the Department of Foreign Affairs in Dublin, looking for a press quote. I was working on a feature about mining exploration for the Belfast Newsletter. We hit it off straight away;I think my kipper tie helped!We didn't want to get married in Dublin and explored other locations as possible options, including Scotland, before we found that we could get married on the Isle of Man with the minimum of notice. It was almost a question of just turning up with no prior waiting. So we settled on Peel, which seemed a very attractive small fishing town on the west coast of the island.

We took the ferry from Dublin to Douglas and then headed across to Peel, where we soon found lodgings with a lovely couple who lived at Victoria Terrace. Arthur Davies had been a postman until he retired. Both he and his wife Ruth hailed from Lancashire, but had been living on the Isle of Man for many years. As soon as they discovered why we were in Peel, they laid on the festivities for us. They were a lovely couple and we all remained good friends until they died, first Arthur, then his wife Ruth.

We were quickly introduced to the vicar of St German's Anglican church in Peel, Rev H. A. McCullough, whom it turned out, had been educated at Trinity College, Dublin. Without any ceremony or hanging around, he arranged for us to get married in his church a couple of days later, after we had sorted some paperwork in Douglas. My sister Kate arrived from London, the only member of either of our families to be present. With herself as bridesmaid and Bob Shimmin, the church warden, as best man, we did the deed in front of the altar. We stayed on in Peel for several more days and got to know the town quite well, along with much of the west and south coast of the island;it was the first of several visits there.

Our wedding was on June 27, 1972, but before then, at Easter, we had gone to Scotland for a few days. We rented a lonely cottage in the hills near Oxton, south of Edinburgh. The cottage itself was fine, but it was the best part of a two mile walk to the nearest bus route, very isolated indeed. But the trip gave us a chance to see a little of the hills of southern Scotland, south of Edinburgh, including the great mansion that was once home to Sir Walter Scott.

1973 Berlin

In January, 1973, barely six months after we had got married, we made our first trip to mainland Europe. Deciding to go to Berlin in the depths of winter was a mad decision and we didn't realise just how mad it was until we arrived there, with a wind howling in from Siberia and daytime temperatures hovering around 20 degrees below freezing.

We'd set off by train from Liverpool Street station in London, going to Harwich, where we caught the ferry to the Hook of Holland. The ferry arrived there late at night and we settled in for the overnight train journey to Berlin. We had one companion in our compartment, a rather charming and overweight Dutchman, who immediately became most attentive towards Bernadette. At one stage along the route, the train stopped for a few minutes at a station somewhere in western Germany, he got off, found a magnificent box of chocolates and returned to present them to Bernadette. She and he chatted for most of the night, while I dozed off. But from the snatches of conversation I heard, it soon became obvious, filling in the gaps in what was left unsaid, that he had been a collaborator with the Germans when the Netherlands was occupied by the Nazis during the second world war. He'd obviously paid the price for this after the war. More excitement came when the East German customs men closely quizzed everyone on the train before it arrived in West Berlin.

But at 7.30 next morning, we arrived at the Zoo station in West Berlin, tired and disshevelled. We soon found the hotel we'd booked into, fairly luxurious but without a trace of the warmth and welcome one would get at any hotel in Ireland. The weather was so bad that we could do little sightseeing in West Berlin. We went to one bar for refreshments and we got a quite stunning surprise. The good looking woman who was the barmaid was topless and seemed entirely unconcerned by her lack of clothes and modesty. In those days, such a display was unheard of in either Ireland or England, but I was transfixed by the conversation I had with the barmaid, whose breasts were almost literally in my face as we talked. Bernadette was merely amused. We saw another sight strange for those times in another pub, where men were seated at the counter, enjoying their beers and what was on a large screen for their benefit-porn films. The drinkers were as engrossed in this as if they were watching horse racing or football!Another night-time excursion was to a nightclub, where the spirit of 1920s Berlin was brought to life, if only in a very modest pastiche. I ended up on stage, doing a dance, remarkably badly;I was lucky after the drink I'd consumed, that I didn't end up flat on my face!

The most interesting part of the trip was going through Checkpoint Charlie into East Berlin. At the checkpoint, everything and everyone on the bus was carefully examined.

East Berlin itself turned out to be remarkably uninteresting, since all we could see were rows of vast, modern blocks of workers' flats. But at least we saw the place before the Berlin Wall came down at the end of the 1980s. We enjoyed refreshments in the restaurant in the building that houses the massive TV tower in East Berlin, but in the end, we were glad to get back to the lights of West Berlin.

We did just one trip outside the city of Berlin, to Potsdam, in its outer suburbs, to visit the great palace of Sans Souci, once the summer home of Frederick the Great, king of Prussia. The palace itself was imposing and we caught glimpses of the Italianate gardens, buried under the snow.

The train from Berlin back to the Hook of Holland had come from Moscow and all the carriages were Russian. In a compartment at the end of each carriage was a huge wood burning stove, designed to keep the passengers warm in winter. Then, eventually, we arrived back in London. We'd seen glimpses of Berlin, enough to whet our curiosity, but the weather had just been too bad to see many of that city's many fascinating places. When we eventually got back to Belfast, where we were then living, it was late at night and all we could hear was the sound of gunfire echoing across the city. In Berlin, there was a pretend peace, but here in Belfast, there was a real war.

1974 Poland

Of all the epic journeys we undertook in the early years of our marriage, Poland was undoubtedly the most interesting. The country was still Communist and we booked for a 14 day bus tour round the country. Getting visas from the Polish travel agency in London was quite a feat, but eventually, we managed it and set off. We travelled from Dún Laoghaire to Holyhead on the ferry;that was straightforward and we arrived on time. But when the train from Holyhead to Euston station in London was halfway through its journey, the engine broke down. We waited for what seemed like hours while a replacement engine was hooked up and we thought by the time we had reached Euston, that catching our flight to Poland would be impossible.

But Gloria, Bernadette's sister, and her husband, Eamonn, had been in London on holiday and they had their VW Beetle car with them. They had turned up at Euston station to meet us from the train and when they found out about the delay, very generously waited for us. Eamonn then drove at breakneck speed to Heathrow airport. We'd also brought quite an amount of luggage with us, but I'd taken tranquillisers for the flight, and was completely incapable of carrying my own luggage. So Eamonn, who very sadly died a decade ago, took over and we finally made the flight to Krakow. We arrived in the middle of the night, to be met with Communist style bureaucracy, but eventually, about four in the morning, we were deposited at our hotel.

The room we were given had lots of mirrors and soon, we sensed that the place was riddled with ghosts, evil ones at that. Only much later did we discover that the hotel had been the Gestapo headquarters during the Germans' second world war occupation of Poland. Many unspeakable atrocities must have taken place there. But apart from the unnerving hotel, we saw plenty of Krakow, including its great cathedral and Wawel castle. As this was a bus trip, it was literally a case of staying in a different hotel in a different town or city every night. We saw the impressive Black Madonna of Czestochowa and we took in an outdoor recital at Chopin's old house, all very interesting. In the city of Poznan in western Poland, while we were taking a ride on an outdoor scenic miniature railway, I managed to catch my thumb in something and bent it back, unbearably painful. That night we went to the local hospital, where I was very expertly X- rayed and bandaged up, all remarkably quickly and all for a payment equivalent to 10p!

Another place we travelled to was Lublin, a city in south-eastern Poland, close to the border with Ukraine. Close to the city was Majdanek, a vast second world war concentration camp, and the tour round it was absolutely harrowing, especially moving because two of the men on the trip with us were two Jewish brothers from London. Only by visiting the camp was it possible to understand the absolute depths of depravity and wickedness to which the human spirit will descend. When we'd arrived at the camp, at the welcome desk, just like any ordinary tourist location, there were racks of greeting cards, showing scenes from the camp, all very macabre. I remember turning to Bernadette and asking what was one supposed to do, send them to people you really dislike and say "having a lovely time, wish you were here".

We also spent some time in Warsaw, where we soon found it was exceptionally cheap. One of the waiters in the hotel we stayed in asked if we'd like to change money, so we stashed a few US dollars underneath our plates, he took them away and a short while later, came back with piles of zlotys. We also noticed in Warsaw that flash queues were forming;just on the mere hint that a shop was getting in supplies, people queued up without knowing precisely what was going to be on offer. In those days, before the Communists were ousted from power, supermarkets were half empty. Another indication of Communist inefficiency came when we checked into what we thought was a modern hotel. We took to lift up about eight or nine floors, only to find when we got out of the lift, only the landing had been built. The room we were supposed to be staying in hadn't even been built!

Fittingly, the charming and efficient woman who was our tour guide for the whole trip round Poland was called Eva and she came from Gdansk, which is were the roots of the rebellion against Communist rule began, in the shipyards.

We were very impressed with the way in which the old town in Warsaw had been meticulously rebuilt;it had been destroyed in 1944. We also had another unusual experience in Warsaw. A guy on the trip was called Chris, a typical London eastender. He was so besotted with Bernadette that he offered us fistfuls of dollars if he could "borrow" Bernadette for a few hours and take her to the Hotel Bristol and shag her silly, but even though we were poor, discretion prevailed and Chris never got the fun-filled hours he was hoping for. Our final stop in Poland was in Novy Sacz, in the far south of the country, in the Alpine region of Poland, and we enjoyed a trip on a large canoe down one of the rushing rivers. Our trip to Poland had come to an end and we'd got a fascinating glimpse into the country.

1975 Brussels, Lucerne, Vienna, Bristol, Edinburgh

We did three particularly memorable trips in 1975, one to Brussels, another to Lucerne and a third to Vienna. Brussels turned out to be a civil servant's paradise, but it did produce some hilarious moments and we did get to taste the famed frites, or chips, that Belgium is renowned for. The journey to and from London to Brussels by train and cross-channel ferry was mundane enough, but the hotel we'd booked, just off the Avenue Louise, was very comfortable and in the bathroom attached to our bedroom, the bath was big enough for two, which created a lot of fun. After you've seen the main square in the centre of Brussels and the Mannekin Pis statue of the little boy peeing, there isn't a lot left to see in Brussels, unless you count the vast office blocks that house various branches of the ultra-bureaucratic European Commission.

But naturally enough, we did discover the street of whores, close to the main railway station, where ladies in various states of undress presented themselves in windows. In Amsterdam, the women in the windows had seemed very robotic and listless, but the Brussels' ladies were much more human, and clearly full of fun and good humour. Some of them were amused that Bernadette and I were walking down the street together and made various obscene gestures, often with a smile or laugh. We also went to see an X rated film in Brussels-it's one way of passing the time of Brussels boredom-and we were very amused by one scene, where a man is in an apartment that is burgled. To save himself, he locks himself in the bathroom and tucks his genitals behind him, so that to all intents and purposes, he looks like a woman. The scene was hilarious and we laughed out loud in the cinema, a rare enough event by any standards!

We also remember vividly one restaurant we visited, for Sunday lunch;the proprietor and chef was Egpytian, a most friendly and charming man and to add to the charm, the restaurant had a house cat, or rather kitten, which was full of fun and most playful and friendly. We had wanted to visit Bruges, which is only a short distance from Brussels, but by this stage, our cash was running low, so we never made it. Overall, my impression of Brussels was that it is bourgeois, boring and bureaucratic and it never created any longings for a return visit.

Lucerne in Switzerland was a complete contrast, a throughly delightful lakeside city, bursting with life and character. We stayed in a modest three star hotel called the Drei Konige (the Three Kings) and it was very comfortable and atmospheric. We loved wandering round the city streets and down by the lakeside, as well as going for pedal boat trips on the Vierwaldstattersee. We also much enjoyed going round the vast transport museum, which has an enormous array depicting all modes of transport, from cars and trains to boats and aircraft. No wonder it's the most popular museum in Switzerland. Something else we saw in Lucerne was the famous carving of the dying lion;it was carved to commemorate the massacre of hundreds of Swiss guards in 1792;they were guarding the Tuileries palace in the centre of Paris when a revolutionary mob overran the place and killed all the Swiss soldiers.

We also walked across the medieval bridge that spans the river in the centre of Lucerne. The Kapellbrucke was built from wood in the 14th century, spanning the Reuss river, and the interior is amazing, lined with medieval paintings. In August, 1993, the bridge caught fire and very serious damage was caused. But with typical Swiss clockwork efficiency, the bridge was completely restored and reopened to the public within eight months. It's a good job the crowd that are doing the Luas cross-city works in Dublin city centre weren't responsible!From Lucerne, we took the railway to the top of Pilatus and we also went sightseeing alongside the Brienzersee, and particularly enjoyed the town of Brienz.

Lucerne of course is in the German-speaking part of Switzerland and that year, our third trip to German speaking lands was to Vienna. That was hilarious because I did my exhibition special again there. A party of Irish bakers had decided to go and have a look at a bakery exhibition in Vienna. I found myself designated the group leader and I also had to write the whole event up. We duly found the bakery exhibition and it turned out to be so slight that I did my whizz round in about 30 minutes flat, yet found plenty to write about when I got home!

That meant we had plenty of time for sightseeing. The bakers weren't too fussed about the exhibition, either, as they too were hellbent on seeing the sights. We explored all the sights of Vienna, including the great cathedral, the Stefansdom. At the time, the new underground railway system was being built in Vienna and we discovered that it was perfectly possible to clamber down and see the work in progress. Other sights in Vienna included the famous riding stables and the royal palace.

We saw the Danube, which is far from blue, more a dirty green. We crossed over a really solid stone bridge, many lanes wide, that spanned the Danube and went to see the Prater pleasure garden with the famous Third Man ferris wheel. A hit song of the time was filling the air, Rod Stewart's Sailing. We were very amazed when, a few months later, that solid looking bridge collapsed into the Danube. We also saw one particular sight in Vienna that was truly horrific. A man was lying on the pavement, having been struck by a vehicle. He looked Turkish and he was immobile, clearly unconscious, on the pavement. A lot of blood was oozing out of his head and the poor man looked as if his fate had already been sealed. We could do nothing for him, as the emergency services had already been called, except continue on our way and say a prayer for his soul.

We also did a trip down to Eisdenstadt, where the great composer worked at the royal palace for so many years. The nearby Neusiedlersee with all its reed beds was fascinating;it's the largest steppe lake in Europe and is home to almost 300 bird species. and we learned that the chimney tops in the nearby village of Rust, a renowned wine place, were well frequented by storks during their breeding season. We also went up close to the nearby border with Hungary, which was still Communist. The border was formidable, a concrete wall topped with barbed wire and peeping over it was the nearest we ever got to seeing Hungary.

The autumn season was in full swing and when we got back to Vienna, we were able to enjoy sunny autumn days on the hillsides of Vienna, enjoying the wine taverns, the heurigen. Then back to dull reality in Dublin, so that I could turn my extremely brief trip round the bakery exhibition into scintillating copy!

On our way to Vienna, we'd had a hilarious experience at Heathrow;in those days, you couldn't fly direct from Dublin to Vienna. We were making our way through Heathrow when we noticed scenes being shot for a film. It was To The Devil A Daughter, based on a Dennis Wheatley novel. One of the production crew asked us if we'd care to be extras for a few minutes, so we did, and we were even more surprised, when a few months later, the film was released. We went to see it in the old Ambassador cinema in central Dublin and there up on screen in glorious technicolour for a few brief moments was the pair of us. We hadn't ended up on the cutting room floor!

That same year also saw a couple of trips to Scotland, of which the most memorable was the one to Edinburgh in December to attend a food festival and sample, all in the interests of work, many memorable Scottish foods. One of the hilarious happenings about Edinburgh that always sticks in my mind was when I was busy photographing the wonderful Georgian architecture in the New Town. Bernadette was standing beside me, holding my open camera bag. A fellow tourist came along and wanted to drop money in the bag-he thought that Bernadette was collecting for charity. She should have told him she was-for us!We also did a trip to Bristol, courtesy of Harvey's Bristol Cream sherry;we were well looked after and well wined and dined. We also enjoyed looking round the hulk of the Great Britain, then newly returned to Bristol. The ship with its iron hull, had been designed and built by Brunel, the great railway engineer and ship constructor;the ship itself was the longest passenger ship in service in the world between 1845 and 1854, but over a century later, was a wreck, abandoned in the Falklands Islands. It was brought back to Bristol in 1970 and when we saw over the hull, restoration work had barely begun.

Also in Bristol, we walked over and admired another piece of Brunel's work in the city, the suspension bridge over the Clifton Gorge. Sir John Betjeman, poet and lover of Edwardian and Victorian England, was quite right:he praised Bristol for being the most interesting city in England, with an architectural heritage to match. But as always, there was a funny side. I remember well, on a subsequent trip, going to a garage in Bristol to collect a van we had rented for our travels round the West Country. The garage manager had a fine dog with him, a Labrador, very friendly and what he said to us has always stuck in my mind. Speaking in a broad West Country accent, he said of his dog:" Don't take any notice of him, he's as daft as a brush".

1976 Champagne and Nice

This year, in July, we made the first of several trips to the Champagne country, a useful spinoff from all the writing I was doing at the time about the drinks trade. In Épernay, we met up with François Bonal, who was the head of publicity for the Champagne houses. He was a formidable host and we were incredibly well looked after. We were housed in the Royal Champagne hotel, which is seven km outside Épernay and on our first night there, we were told to enjoy whatever we wanted from the menus and the wine list. There were three of us in our little party, Bernadette, myself and a drinks trade journalist, appropriately from Glasgow. At dinner that night, we consumed nine bottles of Champagne between us, followed up by a couple of cognacs, just to chase it all down, you understand. The next morning, we woke up in our bedroom, which faced out onto the gardens of the hotel and by 9am, we were out in the vineyards, with our genial host François giving us a running commentary on the state of that year's vines and the likely harvest outcome. In the background was the famous windmill near Épernay. We were all totally clear headed, which was amazing considering what we'd been downing the previous night.

As for François, he was always a formidable host and looked after us extremely well any time we went to Épernay. We became good friends and remained so until his death in 2003. He had been a long time officer in the French army and when he retired, he made a seamless transition to Épernay. No-one proved better at promoting the virtues and values of Champagne and he also wrote many books on the subject. One of his books that we still have at home is his monumental encyclopedia on the subject, with a very apposite gold cover. But François was typically French in another way; he couldn't resist Bernadette's bottom and any chance he got to sneak a feel of its contours, he made the most of!

We toured some of the really posh Champagne houses, such as Moët et Chandon and we also went to see a small family run Champagne house, which was much better fun. The owners and the workers were full of fun, especially as we'd arrived in the middle of a retirement "do" for one of the workers. We also visited Reims, including the majestic 13th century Gothic cathedral. It was more than a bit disconcerting to be in a party going round the cathedral at the same time that a funeral service was being conducted. We felt the incongruity was entirely appropriate.

At the end of that year, we made our first visit to Nice, travelling because of budgetary constraints, with Thomson Holidays, a cheap and cheerful travel experience. The flight from Luton to Nice was uneventful and we found they'd booked us into a three star hotel close to the city centre and the famous Promenade des Anglais. In Nice itself, we enjoyed long walks along the Promenade, created during the 19th century at a time when English aristocrats ruled the roost in Nice; these days it's the Russians. The delightful style, almost innocence, of Nice, was destroyed in a terrorist attack in July, 2016, when close on 100 people were killed along the Promenade.

The restaurants in the old quarter of Nice, when we were there in 1976, were pleasant and agreeable, but altogether, we found that Nice, rather than being a city worth exploring, was better used as a base for touring the region. Travelling west from Nice by train, we got as far as St Tropez, which we enjoyed immensely. It has a vast harbour, which in summer is filled with the yachts of the super rich, but in December, there were few of these to be seen and precious few other tourists. Neither did we see any sign of the town's most famous resident, Brigitte Bardot, film star turned animal rights' activist.

Travelling east from Nice, we came to Antibes, an interesting enough town, where the highlight was the Picasso museum. Then it was on to Monte Carlo, a place we took an instant dislike too-it simply reeked of tax free riches and a quick walk round the centre of this tiny principality cured us of any desire to return. But the town beyond Monte Carlo was a total gem, Menton. In the 19th century, this had been a popular bathing place, and place for better off tourists from England to spend the winter months. Many of its 19th century buildings are still intact, rebuilt after the devastating 1887 earthquake. We also inspected the wonderful medieval St Michel Archange church on the hill beside the harbour in the town. The town has a wonderful fin de siècle atmosphere about it. We were also reminded that just outside Menton, the famous Irish poet W. B. Yeats, died in 1939. It was nearly a decade, because of the second world war, before his remains were repatriated to Ireland and reburied in the graveyard of the Church of Ireland church at Drumcliff, Co Sligo. But legends persist that it wasn't Yeats at all who is buried there, but the remains of a local man from the Menton area.

The last stop on our rail borne itinerary west of Nice was Ventimiglia, the first stop across the frontier in Italy. Since this was Italy, chaos and confusion abounded, but the town was decorated for Christmas and the markets were in full swing;we tried one of the local delicacies, roasted chestnuts.

All too soon, it was time to pull down the curtain on our week in Nice, a most enjoyable introduction to the Cote d'Azur. We clambered aboard the Thomson Holidays' flight at Nice airport, for what we thought would be a routine flight, but it proved anything but. When the plane was taking off from Nice airport, the view in the clear December air was absolutely spectacular. Nice airport is right beside the sea and as the plane climbed, we could see not only the whole of the city of Nice, but almost the whole of the Cote d'Azur, as far as the soaring mountain peaks of the French Alps, 160 km distant. It was truly the most spectacular take-off we've ever seen.

But into the flight, we crossed France without any trouble, then the English Channel, before the pilot came on to say there were problems ahead. There was thick fog in the London area and the plane couldn't land at Luton or anywhere else close to London. He said that he had decided to press on to Birmingham and we were left wondering whether the plane could safely touch down there, and if so, how we were going to get back to Dublin. As luck had it, no sooner had we safely touched down at Birmingham, but we discovered that an Aer Lingus flight was about to depart to Dublin, so in the end, we made a quick getaway.

1977 Lisbon, Jerez de la Frontera, Munich, Salzburg

This was a great year for wine writing! We made two trips that provided lots of interesting copy. The first was in June to Jerez de la Frontera, the sherry making centre in southern Spain. We flew from Dublin to Heathrow and then on to Seville, and a quick trip round the city gave us glimpses of its magnificent architecture, including its cathedral. But the main purpose of the trip was to stay in Jerez de la Frontera and see how sherry is bottled and matured. It was an interesting enough experience, although I can't say I particularly like Spain; it's too hard edged and sharp. However, one of the lunches we had was quite spectacular, at a beachside restaurant at Sanlucar de Barrameda, not far from Jerez. The atmosphere and the searing heat, were quite unforgettable. Equally unforgettable was the dinner we had in Cadiz one night, a dinner replete with loads of fish, rather fittingly. But in true Spanish style, the dinner didn't start until 10pm, so that it didn't finish until well after midnight, by which time, after all the wine, I was all ready to fall face first into the dessert plate!

The second wine related trip came in October and was much more pleasant and interesting. We found people in Portugal much more easy going, very akin to people in Ireland, without the hard-nosed harshness of character that can often be found in Spain. We flew from Paris to Lisbon aboard a TAP flight;most of the passengers were bound for Fatima. Some of these passengers were most unruly-just right for religious pilgrims-so the flight was barely tolerable. But once we'd arrived in Lisbon and checked into our hotel, we set about exploring a really interesting city.

We loved all the hillside landscapes in the city, and the ancient trams that still trundled along. At night we enjoyed the night clubs with women singing fado, the traditional Portuguese song that often forms a lament. In one night club, we struck up a friendship with a very elderly man who had been taken there by his nurse. The man was very interesting and kind to talk to and we found it very sad that the nurse who was looking after him, and was his companion for the night out, had absolutely no interest in him as a person and was merely doing her job for money.

We saw many of the tourist sights of Lisbon, including the great tower of Belem. The whole country was remarkably peaceful and running well, despite the fact that only four years previously, the long fascist dictatorship under Salazar, begun in the 1930s, had been overthrown in favour of democracy. Outside Lisbon, we made one trip across the Tagus river to see the wine making district on the far side of the estuary. But as it was pouring with rain, we could do little except spend the afternoon in a bar!We also took the train from Lisbon to Estoril and Cascais, which are only about 15 km along the coast from Lisbon. Estoril, where so many figures from European royalty had sought refuge during the 20th century, didn't appeal at all, but Cascais was totally different. It was a really interesting seaside town, full of atmosphere and full of lovely restaurants where you can enjoy Portuguese seafood cooking at its best. We had a memorable and wine-laden lunch there!We also journeyed to places along the Atlantic coast, such as Nazaré, to find the beaches full of traditional fishing boats that had been drawn up there.

Our best trip in Portugal was up north, to Porto and the Douro valley, home of port. We did the journey by train from Lisbon to Porto and back again and one thing that struck us very much was the number of men on the trains that were missing limbs. They had all been soldiers in the Portuguese army, who had been fighting various liberation wars in Africa, wars that Portugal inevitably lost.

Porto itself turned out to be a remarkably atmospheric city, built on hillsides overlooking the Duoro river. We saw Vila Nova de Gaia, on the other side of the estuary from Porto and closer to the sea, where all the port companies had their warehouses, prior to their products being shipped out. But as we travelled by car from Porto to the heart of the port country, a distance of about 150 km, we were struck by the extreme poverty of the countryside and of the villages we passed through. We were hosted by Cockburn's port and stayed in their wonderfully exquisite villa overlooking the river. The manager was English, who was addicted to the tune, then popular, Spanish Harlem. As we stood on the balcony at the villa at night- time, looking down on the great Duoro river, he kept dropping hints as to how good a sleeper I was. He was obviously intent on having his wicked will with Bernadette, but we managed to spend our nights, together and by ourselves, beneath the mosquito nets, in the torrid heat.

We also went for a trip along the river in a traditional river boat;the local men who made up the crew, rowed us up and down the river and were most gracious and friendly. At the end of the river trip, they were all delighted to be included in the group photograph. Also in the Douro valley, we inspected one of the vineyards that supplied Cockburns with grapes, which in those days, were all trodden by bare footed workers.

We also met a lovely, friendly black dog, who was thoroughly inebriated. It turned out that the dog had been busy munching away on fermenting grapes these had made the animal thoroughly sozzled. I've never before or since since seen a dog in such a state of drunkeness.

We'd packed a lot into our week in Portugal and when we returned from Porto on the Sunday night, we saw that hundreds of other people were getting off the train. We wondered how on earth we were going to get transport back to our hotel, and then it turned out that there were literally hundreds of taxis at the station ready to take all the passengers from the train. The next day, it was a TAP flight back to Paris and more airborne chaos. But I couldn't help but notice the headlines in the paper being read by the man in the next row of seats:Bing Crosby had died the day before. In those days, long before iPhones, if you went on holiday abroad, it was very easy to stay completely aloof from what was happening elsewhere in the worldl

That year also saw a trip to southern Germany and Austria. I was covering one of those great exhibitions that German industry loves to revel in;personally, I've always found them utterly boring, and out of all the ones in Germany that I had to write up, I always managed to whizz round them at top speed, gather up all the press releases and then when I was home, wrote copy that started:I Was There!But there was always another reason for skating through these vast German exhibition halls in record time;the less time I spent there, the more time Bernadette and myself had for sightseeing. I can't say we particularly enjoyed our trip to Munich in the summer of 1977.

We were well aware of the city's notorious past, as the seedbed of the Nazi conquest of Germany in the early 1930s. Apart from the fine cathedral, we didn't find the other architectural pieces of the city particularly interesting. We didn't even find any area where people could sunbathe in the nude, a great cult in many places in Germany. Neither were we helped in our impressions of Munich by the awful hotel we'd been booked into. Our bedroom was little bigger than an airing cupboard, with not even room to swing a kitten! We hot footed it out of Munich as quickly as we could, heading for the railway station with a great sense of relief.

Munich is 115 km from Salzburg, just over an hour down the line. We arrived somewhere entirely different Salzburg, which we loved, welcome improvement on Munich. We got a humble bed and breakfast place with a Frau Nostiz, on the outskirts of Salzburg. She made us very welcome, in the best Austrian style, and we set about exploring the city, everywhere from the Mirabell Gardens, to the Mozart museum, the Mozart balls (chocolate ones, I hasten to add) and the cathedral. Salzburg we found to be a wholly delightful place, compounded by the bar we went to at night. In their downstairs section, they had traditional Austrian folk music and it was so melodic that it set us tapping our feet and humming the tunes. This was the first time we'd visited Salzburg and we were so taken with the place that in time, a second trip beckoned.

1978 Athens, Channel Islands, Copenhagen, Isle of Man

That year provided some very interesting travel contrasts; on a personal level, we derived much enjoyment from taking Bernadette's parents, Hugh and Mary Quinn, to the Isle of Man to celebrate their 50th wedding anniversary. They had gone to the island for their honeymoon, back in 1928, and had never returned subsequently, so they really enjoyed being back there and seeing all the sights for themselves, including the lovely fishing town of Peel on the west coast, where we had been married in 1972. I should mention at this point that even though Peel is so small, it's correct title is "City of Peel". It has a population of just over 5,000.

The other trip we did that year in this part of the world was to the Channel Islands. I had been there once before, when I was about eight years old, and was taken on a day trip by sea to Guernsey. All I can remember of that particular trip was that I was all dolled up in my Scottish "uniform" in Sinclair tartan, complete with kilt. I must have been a sight to behold! I've had no inclinations in my adult life to go Scottish again, thereby giving rise to the old joke about what's worn under a kilt. "Nothing", is the answer, "It's all in perfect condition". The only other thing I remember about that brief excursion to Guernsey in the early 1950s was that I was so overcome with the plentiful quantities of ice cream on offer that I ate so much of the stuff that I became violently sick!

This particular trip to the Channel Islands was much more comfortable. We flew, in little over an hour, from Dublin to Jersey, where we had booked a hotel on the south side of the island. From the hotel, it was a walk of about two km, via a long tunnel, into the main town and capital, St Helier. We enjoyed wandering round St Helier and dining in some of its restaurants, including Rascal's restaurant, just opposite the main post office. We also hired a mini car, so we were able to drive all round the island, navigating the many small country lanes and exploring in detail the beaches and cliffscapes on the north of the island. We were also fascinated, on our travels round the island, by the adorable Jersey cows that seemed to be peeping over every hedge.

The Channel Islands are easy to travel round, which we did, using Aurigny, a locally based airline. Their small, bright yellow planes were made for island hopping, even if there was precious little room inside them. One of the trips was a day long excursion to St Peter Port, the capital of Guernsey, which I must admit is a much more agreeable and interesting destination than Jersey, too obviously full of bankers and millionaires living in tax free exile.

The main item of interest in St Peter Port was the house where the French writer Victor Hugo, once lived in exile in the mid-19th century. The house is well preserved and full of artefacts relating to him. Later on, we followed this up by going to the extensive Victor Hugo museum in the 3rd arrondissement of Paris.

It's amazing how much you can squeeze into a day trip, when you know that every minute counts and you organise things so as not to waste a precious second. During that day trip to Guernsey, we also managed to nip across to its sister island, Herm, which is renowned for its absolutely fantastic sandy beaches and real "away from it all" atmosphere.

Alderney was a completely different story, another day trip by air from Jersey. During the second world war, the Channel Islands were occupied by the Nazis, none more brutally than Alderney. When we were there, we walked down to the harbour, with its great breakwater. On the surface, it all looked remarkably peaceful, with just a few fishing boats and plenty of seabirds, but the atmosphere there was overwhelmingly evil. It's one of the few places I've been in that reeks of utter depravity and savagery and later, we found out the reason. During the second world war, the Nazis had brought many prisoners to the island from elsewhere in occupied Europe. The conditions they had to endure were as bad in the concentration camps in mainland Europe and many of them died unspeakable deaths in the harbour as they were being brought to and from the island. So the awful feeling of sheer evil was very much in the air when we saw the harbour and it all had a very logical explanation. The rest of Alderney, including its one and only town, St Anne, was interesting enough, but when the plane took off, going back to Jersey, we were highly relieved.

The only one of the Channel Islands we didn't visit was Sark. In the old days, this was renowned for being the most archaic of the Channel islands, devoid of any car traffic, but in recent years, it has become renowned for all the wrong reasons. The Barclay brothers who own the Daily Telegraph newspaper, live in an island castle just offshore from Sark. And in recent years, the island population has been torn apart by many divisive plans to develop it, so that these days, Sark is a much less pleasing place to visit than it used to be. The air there seems filled with acrimony rather than car-free peace and quiet.

We also did a trip by hovercraft from Jersey to St Malo, which gave us virtually the whole day there, plenty of time to explore the lovely seaside setting of the town and cross the river to take a quick look at the more up market town of Dinard.

There was also a reminder of the second world war in the second big trip we did in 1978, to Athens. Again, we went the cheap and cheerful way, with a Thomson Holidays package. We were installed in a modern but modest hotel close to the centre of Athens;the last night we there, Bernadette woke me up to say that she could see the ghost of a woman sitting at the dressing table, fixing her make-up in the mirror. I could see nothing, but certainly felt a shivery atmosphere. It turned out that an old theatre had previously existed on the site of the hotel and that perhaps what we were seeing was a ghost from the period of the second world war, when the Greeks enduring frightful hardships at the hands of the Nazis. After the Nazis came the Brits, as the country was riven by civil war, and by all accounts, they weren't much better. In recent years of course, the Germans have been back in another guise, the painful budgetary disciplines imposed on the Greeks at the behest of the Germans.

Modern day Athens wasn't particularly interesting, apart from the Parthenon and the 1896 Olympic stadium, where the first of the modern Olympics was staged. So we spent as much time as we could out of the city, taking trips to neighbouring islands. The island we enjoyed most was Aegina, about an hour's boat trip from Pireaus. We took a trip round the island in a donkey cart;the driver was an elderly man with little or no English, but he was very charming, and was delighted to show us all the orchards laden with fruit and the interior of the island, totally unspoiled by development. The main town on the island, with the same name as the island, has a lovely harbour setting and we enjoyed an al fresco lunch in a quayside restaurant. We went on another day trip to a more distant island, Póros, which with its houses piled up on the hillsides, looked much more like a traditional Greek island. We befriended a very sick and scrawny looking cat and found it some fish to eat, but it was in such bad condition that it just sicked the lot up. Close to Athens, we went to the island of Piraeus and found the main town, Salamis, by the seaside, interesting enough, despite the hideous sight on the quayside. A fisherman was beating the bejasus out of an octupus, on the stones of the quayside, to make it ready for a nearby restaurant. Ugh!We also took a long bus trip out of Athens as far as Corinth. The route passes over the Corinth Canal, a remarkable construction that we were able to get a good sight of. We also took a trip south-east of Athens, to Sounion, to see the remarkably preserved Temple of Poseidon.

Closer to Athens, we find another good spot to hang out, some of the coffee places in Glyfada, close to Athens airport, and it was a great way of spending an hour or two, watching the incoming planes flying so low as they approached the airport. But one other excursion we planned didn't come off:we had wanted to visit the island of Hydra, which is a two hour boat journey from Athens. It's a famed tourist destination, among the most renowned of the Greek islands, but the young man on the desk in our hotel in Athens made a complete cock-up of booking the taxi we needed to make the boat for Hydra, an early morning departure.

We also found that Athens was a culinary disaster;we tried a couple of recommended restaurants for our evening meals and found them to be a total disaster. Then we lighted upon the Hotel Grande Bretagne, right in central Athens, almost next to the parliament building with its ceremonial guard dressed in traditional Greek fighting uniform. The hotel was and still is one of the poshest in Athens, but we found we could have very pleasant meals there for a reasonable price. We had one amusing incident there;one night, when we were leaving, we got into conversation with one of the concierges. He was very polite but not very forthcoming;he obviously thought we were English from somewhere in the home counties. We told him that we lived in Dublin and were going back there at the end of our holiday. His whole demeanour changed in an instant;like many Greeks, he disliked the Brits almost as much as he despised the Germans. The concierge was well up on Irish history, which Greeks closely identify with, and in a whoop of delight, shouted out the name of Ireland's best known politician of the 20th century, Eamon de Valera.

At the end of 1978, we made another continental trip, which like the earlier one to Berlin, didn't turn out to be such a good idea at all, because of the appalling weather. We went to Copenhagen immediately after Christmas with the intention of seeing in the New Year there. But the weather was so bad that we saw little of the city's sights, except for a few exceptions, like the statue of the mermaid. But we did get to Roskilde and saw the Viking museum there, which was very interesting, and the nearby Kronberg castle, which was the model for Elsinore in Shakespeare's Hamlet. We also took the ferry, in very stormy conditions, across to the the southern Swedish city of Malmö, where we could do little because of the weather except down drinks in a hotel bar.

1979 Lake District and Normandy

In June, 1979, we journeyed via Liverpool to Kendal, to explore the Lake District, a part of the world we hadn't known before. We stayed in the hotel close to the railway station in Kendal, where we were well looked after and where we ate and drank well;Kendal turned out to be an exceptionally pleasing town, which we much enjoyed. During our stay in the Lake District, we noted an historical turning point;in the UK general election, Margaret Thatcher became British prime minister for the first time. We always remember seeing and hearing her first speech as PM, on the steps of Number 10, Downing Street, wonderfully aspirational and totally delusional, mere political rhetoric that was never translated into action. She had said in that speech, quoting St Francis of Assisi, "where there is discord, let there be harmony". She went on to create an enormous amount of political discord.

But in the pleasing landscapes of the Lake District, what was happening in London's political life seemed thankfully remote. We enjoyed travelling through the area, including Windermere, to admire the vast lake, the largest in England, and Keswick. We enjoyed visiting Wordsworth's Dove Cottage, at Grasmere. The cottage is 400 years old and right next door is the equally fascinating museum. We also went as far as Whitehaven on the Cumbrian coast, a complete contrast, it was such a desolote and drab industrialised seaside town.

Our other trip that year was more dramatic, to Trouville in Normandy. We travelled by train from Dún Laoghaire to Rosslare and took the Irish Continental Lines' ferry to Le Havre. The overnight journey was tedious and uncomfortable, as the seas were running high. But once we got to Le Havre, we made our way to Trouville, across the Tancarville bridge until then spanned the estuary of the Seine. It was eventually replaced by the epoch design of the present bridge, opened to traffic in 1995. When we landed in Trouville, we knew we'd hit a gem of a seaside town. We soon found somewhere to stay, the small Hotel St James;our room was small and the bathroom was poky, but it was perfectly comfortable and it had a great attraction;the owner was an addicted cat lover and owned about half a dozen lovely mogs, who at breakfast time, would sit on the table watching us munch our croissants. It was a wholly delightful way to start the day.

Trouville still had the atmosphere of a traditional fishing port and when we where there, it had lost none of that vitality. We also had tremendous fun in a restaurant in the town centre called Les Vapeurs, a traditional seafood restaurant, absolutely bursting with atmosphere, joie de vivre and good cooking. Two evening visits there were wholly delightful and I'm glad to say that the place is still going strong. Late at night, after our evening meal, we developed a routine of going for a walk along les planches, the boardwalks by the beach. It was pitch dark and the only sound was of the sea rolling in;these days, we wouldn't consider doing such night time walks, but in those days, it was reasonably safe.

Just across the river from Trouville is Deauville, which by comparison, is a right pain in the proverbial. Deauville is all about the moneyed rich, a sure way to ensure that any atmosphere is drained from the place. The rich always spoil anywhere they swarm;just look at Monaco. It was the same in Deauville;we couldn't summon up any liking for the place at all and even through the promenade has a great stretch to it, ideal for a long walk, it had none of the pleasant atmosphere we found in Trouville.

In a westerly direction, we travelled along the coast by bus, through rather dreary places like Dives and Houlgate, until we reached Cabourg. The front there is very atmospheric and we could see immediately why Proust, the author of his mythical remembrances, À la recherche du temps perdu, enjoyed it so much. It was his favourite place for summer vacations and his fictitious Balbec is based on Cabourg. But on a personal level, it was marred by the mosquito infestation;Bernadette was badly bitten by them, although I must have some inbuilt aversion to them, because the little critters never came near me. In the other direction from Trouville, going back towards Le Havre, we found another absolutely delightful spot, Honfleur.

This medieval seaside town still has much of its 18th century quayside architecture and a walk around the quaysides was most rewarding, along with a visit to St Catherine's medieval church. Honfleur is such a rewarding spot that in summer time, it's a huge tourist attraction, but because we were there in October, the crowds were much thinner. This had been our first trip to Normandy and overall, we enjoyed it greatly, with the exception of Deauville, that miserable, bleak place with the rarified atmosphere generated by the super rich and indolent. We also had a very uncomfortable trip back to Rosslare because the seas were so rough. At one stage, a young boy on the ship managed to catch his hand in a steel door and amid the tempest, a rescue helicopter came to the ship from Cornwall and winched the young fellow aboard. But by the time we reached Rosslare, our gait was really rolling and we still felt very queasy from the tempestuous seas.

That trip was also memorable in another way. I had been doing a lot of travel writing for the excellent Cara magazine, the Aer Lingus inflight publication, and with those to offer by way of credentials, I made contact with The Irish Times and a wonderful man called John Butler, who was then running the weekend travel section. He took me on and the first piece I wrote for the paper was on that trip to Normandy. John, who was a marvellously sympathetic travel editor to work for, a most civilised man, died in 2013.

1980 Boston, Luxembourg, Normandy

This was an exceptional travel year for us; the first trip, in April, came about totally unexpectedly. At the time, I was doing a lot of feature writing for Cara, the Aer Lingus inflight magazine. One day, a phone call from one of the staff, John Allen, once a close neighbour of Bernadette's in Rialto Drive, Dublin, informed me that they had managed to lose a set of transparencies I'd provided for them. In lieu, John offered two return tickets from Dublin to New York.

At the time, New York was in the grip of a transport strike, so we opted instead for Boston, the most Irish city in the US, and it proved a fine choice. We flew from Dublin to Shannon, for the obligatory touch-down there, before heading across the North Atlantic. There were plenty of empty seats on the plane, so we soon found ourselves upgraded to first class. Crossing the Atlantic, there was little to see, until Newfoundland and northern Canada came into view, our first glimpse of the New World. We eventually touched down in Boston and set about finding ourselves a hotel. We booked into a temperance hotel on Massachusetts Avenue in the city, put up with the fact it didn't have any booze, but soon found an alternative hotel right in the city centre, at Copley Square.

We did all the obligatory sights in Boston, including Boston Common, Beacon Street and the city's then tallest building, the John Hancock Tower. Boston was a very congenial place and we soon discovered an even more congenial event. Walking downtown one day, we spotted a notice for a university style revue at a small theatre;there was one small difference, it was going to be performed entirely in the nude. Naturally drawn in, we booked a couple of tickets and made our way to the theatre that night with mounting excitement. All the cast, male and female, were in the nude, and they were doing their take on the day's news, which was very funny, so much so that the big black lady sitting on one side of me was laughing so much that the entire row of seats shook so much we feared it was going to collapse.

The funniest bit however came at the end of the show, where members of the cast, still in the nude, were in the lobby to the theatre to greet theatregoers as they came out of the auditorium. Two rather elderly ladies got into earnest conversation with one of the male leads, entirely ignoring the fact that his rather prominent member was dangling just inches from them. They commented on the actor's surname, which was Polish, and they surmised that his ancestors had probably come from the same place in Poland that their own grandfather had come from.

Also in Boston, we went to see the house in Brookline where John F. Kennedy had grown up and were fascinated by the exuberant collection of memorabilia. We had lunch nearby and all I can remember of that day is that the black waitress who served us was bursting out of her uniform, an unforgettable sight. Then we went to the Kennedy Memorial Library, with even more material about the one-time US President, assassinated in 1963. Outside Boston, we took a bus one rainy afternoon down to Cape Cod and Plymouth, to see where the Pilgrim Fathers had landed in 1620. Also nearer Boston, much nearer, was Cambridge and Harvard Square.

While the outward flight to Boston had been relaxed and comfortable, the return night flight was the exact opposite, packed, with no room to move and highly uncomfortable. Sleep proved extremely elusive. We landed at Shannon at 5.30am in the morning and promptly ordered two Irish coffees to provide some fortification. Eventually, we made it back to Dublin airport and then home, but it took a week for the jet lag from the return air journey to wear off. It had been the exact opposite when we had landed in Boston;with the time difference, we were able to head out for a second dinner the night of our arrival. But all in all, it was a most interesting trip, our only excursion to the US.

A few days after we'd arrived back, another phone call from Aer Lingus;the missing transparencies had been located. But very fortunately, it was after rather than before our trip!

A couple of months after that trip to Boston, we headed to Dusseldorf for another of those interminably boring German trade exhibitions, before we managed to escape and head for Luxembourg. I'd checked a list of hotels there well before we left, and booked a likely looking hotel by post-in those days, emails were well into the future. When we arrived at the station in Luxembourg, we headed for the hotel, which seemed pleasant enough from the outside. The room too was quite pleasant, although the sheets weren't too clean. Then we paused in the bar and it soon became obvious that this was anything but an hotel-this was a full scale brothel, occupied by various ladies of "leisure". We beat a hasty retreat from what could have been a much too interesting situation!

We rather liked Luxembourg, despite its diminutive size;outside the city, we explored the country's wine district, alongside the River Moselle, and then took another short trip down south to Esch-sur-Alzette, a steel making town in the south of the country. We spent part of a rather wet Sunday afternoon enjoying drinks in the colonnades of a restaurant overlooking the main square. We satisfied our curiosity by walking down a country lane just outside town, to stray into France, without a sign of any frontier crossing.

The third trip that year was in September/October, as far as Normandy, made via a very sea crossing to Cherbourg. We didn't think that Cherbourg itself was any great shakes, so we were glad to leave it for Valognes, an entirely different tourist destination, just 20 km to the south. The town had been virtually destroyed in the aftermath of the 1944 Allied invasion of France, but had been rebuilt so meticulously that it was as if the old town centre had never been touched by war.

We found an excellently comfortable hotel in the town centre, while another nearby hotel, the portentiously named Grand Hotel du Louvre, provided some exceptional evening meals, our plates absolutely laden with food. There was hardly a tourist in sight, which made it even more authentic, and we got into conversation, in French, with various local people, including a fertiliser salesman who came from St Brieuc, much further west along the northern Normandy coast. Some evenings, we also enjoyed sitting on the terrace of a local ice cream parlour, watching the world go by. We also much enjoyed a recital of harpsichord music at the local big house, the Hotel Beaumont.

One small incident in Valognes was rather amusing. One day, as we walked into the town centre from the railway station, an elderly man rushed in front of us, stood in front of a wall that was right beside us, opened his trousers and let fly. He had obviously been bursting with a pee and it was all so natural that we didn't bat an eyelid!

From Valognes, we got as far as the wonderful seaside town of Barfleur, at the tip of the Cotentin peninsula, while in the other direction, saw the famous tapestry in Bayeux and the rebuilt city of Caen. Yes, that trip to Normandy was memorable in many ways and most enjoyable, especially the cats on the breakfast table in Trouville, and it has given us a life-long respect for Normandy and its traditions.

1981 Germany

Not very much travelling this year, except to Germany for another bloody trade exhibition. At this stage, I was getting very fed up with having to cover all these exhibitions in Germany, which I always found to be an incredible bore. No doubt they were of much interest to the business people they were aimed at, but having to cover them as a journalist was incredibly tedious. But at least they gave us a chance to see parts of Germany that we wouldn't have gone to otherwise.

The first place we explored was Cologne, where we climbed to the top of the cathedral. It's a very impressive medieval building dating from the 13th century. It was started in 1248, work stopped in 1473 and it wasn't resumed until the 19th century and completed in 1880. Its spires are the second tallest in Europe. There was an incredible climb up stone steps, all 509 of them to a viewing platform 100 metres above ground level. We were relatively young and energetic then, so we made it to the top without too much puffing and panting, to be rewarded with spectacular views over the roof of the cathedral, the River Rhine, which flows close to the cathedral, and of the city of Cologne itself. Just in front of the cathedral on New Year's Eve, 2015, notorious mass sex attacks by migrants were carried out on many women attending the festivities and these days, the area in front of the cathedral is well sealed off.

The next two stops had far darker connotations. Nuremberg was the place where Nazi rallies took place in the 1930s and we found that there was still an air of foreboding in the air.

The final stop on this miniature odessey in southern Germany was Bayreuth. We had a look round the vast 19th century opera house where the Wagner festivals are staged each year, and at the old 18th century theatre in the town, one of the finest Baroque theatres in Europe, both very interesting buildings. But the place that really got to us was the Wahnfried, what had been Wagner's house, which is now a museum, set in beautiful gardens. All the exhibits there, including all the old photographs, were exceptionally interesting and I especially remember the two of us sitting down to watch a short film of the famed Norwegian soprano, Kirsten Flagstag (1895-1962), singing Wagner;she was one of the most distinguished Wagnerian sopranos. As we sat there on a brilliantly sunny afternoon, outside, through the great windows, we could see all the dinny joes (flower heads) drifting down on the breeze. It was a magical moment, but despite the idyylic setting we couldn't help but think of all the inspiration that Wagner had given the Nazis and how subsequently, various members of his family had been closely involved with them.

In an ironic twist, when we were staying in an extremely comfortable hotel in the centre of Bayreuth, we turned on the television news one night to see footage of the famous reconciliation between France and Germany. The presidents at that time were Mitterand and Kohl respectively, and they were pictured holding hands in a gesture of conciliation in one of the wartime cemeteries in Verdun.

1982 London

This year was mostly memorable for a trip to London, when The Irish Times decided to launch the travel section in its weekend review, at Ireland House in New Bond Street, London, in June, 1982, with the aim of attracting London-based travel companies and organisations as well as airlines. We decided to make a trip of it and go to London under our own steam and enjoy the launch. I remember vividly that the late and much missed Maeve Binchy, made a great speech that was very funny. At that stage, she was a full-time journalist with The Irish Times, but before she started having huge success with her novels. We had a most enjoyable conversation with her and she was very encouraging to me, as I'd just started making travel contributions to the paper. After the event was concluded, John Butler, who was then editing the travel section, took the two of us to a rather vinous lunch nearby, which was most enjoyable. We got to know John much better;he was a most delightful and civilised companion and when he discovered that Bernadette had written a lot of poetry, he encouraged her to send in a couple of samples to the paper, which were duly used.

1983 Scilly Isles, Plymouth, Bath, Bristol, Austria, Lichtenstein

During the summer of that year, we visited the West Country in England, staying in a quaint b & b in Falmouth, that delightful seaside town in Cornwall. The b & b was allright but no great shakes;we found that practically everyone else staying there was well into old age, so we were surrounded by very elderly people. But Falmouth was quite a good base for getting round.

One spectacular trip we did was to Penzance and the Scilly Isles. We did a day trip to Hugh Town, the main town, indeed the only town on the Scilly Isles. It has a population of 1,000, while that for all the inhabited Scilly Isles is a mere 2,200. We flew by helicopter from near Penzance;mercifully, the crossing was very short, about 20 minutes, because the helicopter was so noisy that it was impossible to hold a conversation inside it. A short time later, one of those helicopters came down in the sea just off the Scilly Isles and most of those on board were killed. The helicopter we'd been on had been taken out of service for repairs and the replacement machine had come down in the sea, in thick fog, on July 16, 1983. A total of 20 people were killed;only six survived.

But we enjoyed wandering round Hugh Town, population 1,000, and saw the whole town within the space of an hour or so, followed up by a most delightful and vinous lunch. I've always been attracted to the Scilly Isles, their distance from so-called civilisation, yet home to a fair-sized settlement. They are also in the Gulf Stream, so they get pretty good weather too, including in winter. This particular trip was a big improvement on the first I made to the Scilly Isles, when I was a young child, living in Plymouth. All I can remember of that trip was that we went across on the ferry and that the weather was so rough, I was violently sick!

In this particular trip, we also took in Plymouth, the city where I was born and spent my first few years. But this time, it didn't particularly appeal. The city centre, brand new after the second world war, had once been pristine white, but by this time, it had got very grubby looking and the thing I can remember most about the place was the sheer quantity of graffiti. But this trip also took in Bristol, always worth revisting, and Bath, with all its 18th century Georgian buildings, which we thoroughly enjoyed, including lunch in a restaurant with a very neat device, a clock that went backwards.

In December that year, just after I'd launched my first book on Irish newspaper history, we took off again, this time for a winter holiday in Austria. We enjoyed all the snow, staying in resorts like Kitzbuhl, Mayrhofen and Seefeld. We enjoyed going to the top of the mountains and taking a drink or two I the mountain top bars and watching everyone else ski off the mountain tops, including children. One resort we particularly enjoyed was Mayrhofen, where we stayed in a hotel with a very traditional Austrian design.

One night, we went to one of the night clubs and had a lot of fun dancing in our snow boots, which is actually much easier than it sounds. At the time, the Police were all the rage, so their music made for lively times. Their song that was being played that night was Every Breath You Take, a memorable musical memento.

Our final stop was in Innsbruck, where we had a brief chance to look at the main shopping streets, very traditional in those days, and at its riverside. We also went to a town up in the Alps, very close to Innsbruck, called Igls, a traditional ski-ing village. Bernadette had been there with one of her friends in the early 1950s and we went to the house where she had stayed and met the head of the family, Herr Gruber. In 30 years, he had aged a lot of course, but he still remembered Bernadette and told us how much Igls had changed in the intervening years.

At the end of the trip to Austria, we left Innsbruck by train and crossed the border into Switzerland, briefly, before getting the bus to go to Vaduz, the capital of Lichtenstein. We spent one night there and between that evening and the following morning, we had seen all the sights the town had to offer, including its royal castle. But we didn't see any sign of the factories making false teeth, the tiny principality's main export. But we did see an abundance of brass plates on doors, for companies that had set up subsidiaries here to avail of the tax opportunities. Vaduz has a mere 5,000 inhabitants, the whole of Lichenstein just 37,000. It's one of only two doubly landlocked countries in the world.

The dinner we had that night in the hotel was pleasant enough, with some folk music added for good measure, but as I say, the tourist possibilities of Lichtenstein were quickly exhausted. Then we travelled onwards, for our flight home from Geneva to Dublin. It had been a most interesting and enjoyable trip. I can't say that I've ever particularly enjoyed trips we've done in Germany, but in German-speaking Austria, it's an entirely different ball game.

1984 France, Spain Switzerland and Austria

This was our peak year for travels in Europe, beginning with our trip to France in April. We had tickets for unlimited free travel on SNCF and we made the most of them by doing a circular trip by train round the whole of France.

The journey began with a flight to London Gatwick, with the long defunct airline, Dan Air, then onwards from there to Montpellier. On the approach to Gatwick, when we were both a little sozzled from all the inflight Champagne, the pilot invited us to sit in the jump seats at the back of the cockpit, so that we had a grandstand view of the runway at Gatwick as we came into land. I'm sure that this is against all modern day in flight regulations, but it was fun at the time. Dan-Air closed down in 1992, merged into British Airways.

As the plane came into land at Montpellier, we saw an entirely different sight, masses of pink flamingoes that live on the marshes not too far from the airport. In Montpellier itself, we stayed at the very modern Sofitel right in the city centre. We enjoyed seeing the combination of 19th century and ultra modern architecture around the city centre in Montpellier.

Then it was time to start our train travels, first stop Avignon, where we admired the exterior of the Palais des Papes. Construction started in the 13th century and during the 14th century, the Popes were in residence and Avignon rather than Rome was the centre of the Catholic church. Avignon, with its vast central square, was a fascinating town, but rather than stay there, we picked on a small town called Villeneuve les Avignon, about five km across the river. The main hotel there was most comfortable, suitably upmarket;Le Prieuré had once been a cardinal's palace and a priory, hence its name. We had a splendid dinner the evening we arrived at a restaurant in the town centre, where, for the first time in my life, I tasted aubergines. In one respect, the dinner was too much for us;when we returned to the hotel, Bernadette insisted on having a bath in the large and luxurious bath, and I left her to it. A while later, when I heard no sounds coming from the bathroom, I went in to investigate and found that she had fallen asleep in the bath, with the water running. The water had filled the bath, right up to the level of the overflow, and she was fast asleep in the bath, in dire danger of plunging beneath its waters, but fortunately, I was able to wake her up and alert her to the great peril she was in.

In Villeneuve, we clambered up and around the old castle and generally enjoyed the ambience of the town, far quieter and tourist free than its near neighbour. We also went to the Avignon side of the river bank and walked along what was left of the famous bridge spanning the river. These days, only four spans of the bridge are left, but the song remains, Sur le pont d'Avignon, sung by generations of schoolchildren, not just in France but in England, too. The official name of the half-bridge across part of the Rhone is the Pont Saint-Bénézet.

It was time to move on and take the train to Paris, which we crossed to get to the Gare de l'Est and the train to Épernay, for another brief visit to see our great friend in Champagne, Col Bonal, as always, the exquisite host. Then back to

Paris again, to take another train, this time to Granville in Normandy. While we were there, we managed to see nearby towns like St-Lo and Coutances, both badly damaged during the second world war, but masterfully rebuilt, with remarkable authenticity. As for Granville itself, it had a jolly seaside atmosphere, but on the Saturday, we found the amplified pop music blaring at full volume from loudspeakers strung up on the lamp posts a bit overpowering.

But soon, these two restless travellers were on their way again. We took an hour long boat journey from Granville to the Chausey Islands, which lie about halfway between the western coast of the Cotentin peninsula and Jersey. At low tide, there are 365 islands, but when the high tides common to this part of the world surge in, that number shrinks dramatically, to 52. We landed on the main island, the Grand Ile, had a quick walk around to get a glimpse of its natural beauty and see in the distance the great chateau restored in the 1920s by the man who founded the Renault car company, Louis Renault.

We discovered a modest enough looking farmhouse that served lunch for visitors to the island and were soon enjoying a suitable wine-soaked farmhouse- style lunch, with ourselves the only non-French people in the party. The lunch was long and most enjoyable and after most of the other people had drifted away after lunch, we got into conversation with the woman of the house, the lady who had cooked such a wonderful lunch. At first, she told us how she was so used to life on this isolated island that she only rarely went to what she called the mainland, to do some occasional shopping, and that life there didn't appeal to her at all.

Then came the heart breaking revelation. She told us that a couple of years previously, their young grandson, who was all of two years old, had been staying with his parents, at the farmhouse. For a brief moment, he had been let out of sight, and when his parents went looking for him, they found the little child lying face down in a pool of water. They fished him out, but all attempts at resuscitating him failed. His grandmother remained utterly distraught at the loss of her grandchild and she made no secret of the depth of her loss and her inability to reconcile herself to such a loss. We sympathised with her as best we could.

Back to the mainland, in Granville, and then onwards to our next destination, Mont St Michel. We walked across the causeway to the Mount and when we got onto the island, strolled past the famous restaurant of Mère Poulard, whose name has been given to a brand of biscuits famous in France. We stayed the night in a hotel halfway up the narrow main street;it was incredibly quiet and early the next morning, we could see from our room, the tides sweeping in across the vast area of sand that surrounds the island. After breakfast, we climbed the rest of the way, to the abbey perched at the very pinnacle of Mont St Michel.

From Granville, we took an almost empty Sunday afternoon train back to Paris, where we had intended to linger for a day or two, but we couldn't find an hotel with rooms free in the seventh arrondissement where we wanted to stay, so it was back to the railways. We took the next train to Orleans, where we felt sure we'd find a suitable hotel. We checked into the local Sofitel, which was anything but pleasant. The room we stayed in was dirty and smelled of stale drain water, a most unpleasant experience. Despite Orleans' connections with Joan of Arc, the Maid of Orleans, we felt no inclination to linger and carried on by train to the next stop on our itinerary to a much more pleasant destination, Poitiers.

The hotel there was basic, but clean and comfortable and the dinner was excellent. We had a quick wander round Poitiers and found it a most agreeable town, laden with bookshops, which we thought was a most encouraging sign. Then back to the train and a quick glimpse of Bordeaux as the train crossed the Garonne river. These days of course,

Bordeaux has a fine new tourist attraction, its brand new wine museum. The train travelled further south, through Les Landes, the sandy coastal strip south of Bordeaux, until we arrived in Biarritz.

Here we soon found accommodation at the Hotel Windsor, where like the hotel in Trouville I mentioned in the 1978 entry, the lady owner was also inordinately fond of animals, this time dogs. The place was awash with pet pooches, who were all very friendly. The name of the hotel was of course a clue to the many connections that Biarritz once had with visiting royalty, from England and elsewhere. The beach and the seaside walks over the rocks are all most impressive and one of our treasured prints is one of the famous Picasso painting of the three bathing beauties on the beach at Biarritz, with the tall and undoubtedly phallic lighthouse on the promontory in the background. One morning in Biarritz, when I was out for a walk, I spotted two fine looking young women sitting on a wall near the beach, sunning themselves. They were topless and both had admirable figures. Being a polite sort of person, I greeted them with my customary early morning salutations, which they frostily ignored.

Also in Biarritz, we had a strange encounter in a bookshop, which had a lot of travel books on display, including of course, many under the Michelin imprint. Sitting on top of the display was an impressive plastic model of Bibendum, the Michelin man, standing close to 30 cm tall. We took an immediate shine to the "statue" and when no-one was looking, we quietly purloined him and made a rapid exit from the shop, with him hidden under our jackets. No-one saw us;just as well, as otherwise we might have been in big trouble, but to this day, Bibendum from Biarritz has had a suitable resting spot at home.

From Biarritz, it was the last stage of our marathon train journey round France, which had lasted a fortnight. We got fleeting glimpses of Pau and then of Lourdes, with its basilica, before finally shipping up in Toulouse. We overnighted there in a plain but comfortable hotel in the city centre, but we weren't in the city long enough to form any definite impressions, other than its sheer size. The next morning, we were off again, back by train to Montpellier, to catch our plane home. The fortnight's tour of France by train had been at times exhausting, but it gave us good insights into many parts of the country.

By June, we were all set for more travels, this time to Spain. We based ourselves in Madrid, which we didn't particularly enjoy, partly because of the intense heat, around 45 degrees C in the midday sun. It was unbearably hot and if you sat on a seat on public transport, you literally stuck to it. I had one rather embarrassing experience on the metro in Madrid. It was so hot that I was wearing shorts, but what I was wearing underneath wasn't holding everything in. I was sitting on the Metro, minding my own business as usual, when Bernadette drew my attention to the fact that a lady sitting opposite had her mouth wide open in astonishment. It seemed as if, unknown to me, all my equipment had popped out and was giving her an eyeful, so I hastily rearranged myself!

Madrid has some interesting places, such as the Royal Palace, the Buen Retiro park and the Prado museum with its incredible collection of El Greco paintings.

But that trip was much more interesting for the three trips we did out of the city, rather than our excursions in the Spanish capital. The most interesting visit was to El Escorial, about 40 km from Madrid, which was once the royal town. The remnants of the royal palace with its magnificent library are still perfectly preserved but what was particularly interesting was seeing the vaults where the various deceased members of the Spanish royal family were buried, coffins piled upon coffins, a timely reminder of one's own mortality. Also in El Escorial, we were also very struck by an extravagant poster for an upcoming concert in the town by Victoria de los Ángeles, the renowned Spanish soprano.

We also went to Toledo, which played a key role in the Spanish civil war, when at the start of that war, in 1936, the garrison in the Alcázar or great fort that dominates Toledo defied an onslaught by Republican soldiers to provide a famous Nationalist victory. Franco, the Spanish dictator, had died in 1975, just nine years before this visit we made to Spain, when democracy was still very young, but the dreary, suffocating influence of the Franco era was still heavy in the air in Toledo. We also saw the cathedral and went to see the studio of El Greco, that great but tortured painter. Toledo was of course once an Arab city, going back, some 1,500 years and many traces of those distant times remain today,. We also went to Segovia, which was much more pleasant in a more low key manner. It's on the plains of old Castile and we were intrigued especially by the very impressive Roman aqueduct.

By September, we were off again, this time to Switzerland, where we stayed in Lausanne. We had booked into the Beau Rivage, Hotel, mainly because we had taken the advice of a well-known travel writer in the Daily Telegraph, Nigel Buxton. His description of the place and our experience of the hotel were totally different and I could only conclude that he'd been busy enjoying a freebie there, which drew an ecstatic review from him. The gourmet dinner in its restaurant was supposed to have been the last word in haute cuisine, but it didn't even come near a first word, a ghastly meal from start to finish. When we got home, I wrote a vigorous letter of complaint to the manager, with a long list of faults that we had found. I was rather surprised when we were given a full refund, but I've never had any inclination to return.

We promptly moved to an infinitiely more agreeable hotel, the Chateau d'Ouchy, down by the waterside, where the manager was an Irishwoman, very friendly and helpful. Among the sights we saw in Lausanne was a highly impressive exhibition of Impressionist paintings at the Fondatiom de l'Hermitage.

At that time, as well, I was doing a lot of work for the Berlitz travel guide company, then based in Lausanne, although subsequently it moved to Oxford, England, and then to the US. These days, rather sadly, few people seem to consult printed guide books, preferring such online outlets as Trip Advisor. But I sometimes wonder about people finding out all they can online about their chosen holiday destination before they leave;I think it's often better and a lot more fun to just get the essentials from a guide book and then get immersed in an investigative quest on arrival.

Another highlight of that trip was taking one of the steamers across the lake to Evian les Bains, on the French side, where we spent a night, returning the next day on the steamer.

Back on Swiss soil, we made a return visit to Lucerne, which I think is one of the most pleasant holiday resorts anywhere in Europe. We spent some time in Montreux, home of the famous jazz festival, and went to Berne, the federal capital of Switzerland, which we thought as dull as ditchwater. After we'd checked into our hotel in Berne, we had to make a hasty exit, because all the bed linen was dirty and no-one had got round to changing it. Mind you, on another occasion, we found exactly the same problem at one of the big hotels in Geneva. No-one connects the Swiss with slovenliness and dirt, but here were two examples right under our noses.

One of the most haunting moments of that trip was visiting the new grave at Celigny, between Geneva and Lausanne, where the great actor Richard Burton had been buried a short while before. He had lived in the village for a number of years before collapsing at dying at the age of 58, having burned himself out through an addiction to women, including Elizabeth Taylor, and to drink. But his saving grace was his voice;hearing him recite or play a part was electrifying. I did a poignant piece about his new grave, accompanied by

On Our Way

a Shakesperian quotation rom Hamlet about how flights
of angels sing thee to thy rest, and took some photographs
as well. The piece duly appeared in that excellent women's
magazine in Dublin, Image, which I'm happy to relate is still
going strong.

At home in Dublin that summer, we soon geared up for
yet another trip once autumn had kicked in. We decided we
wanted to go and see Salzburg, but in those days, getting there
was much more complicated. It was impossible then to fly
direct from Dublin, so we had to go via Heathrow. In those
far-off days, we used to go to London quite often, something
I've absolutely no wish to repeat nowadays. We stayed in an
excellent basement flat in Belsize Square, which was just round
the corner from Lancaster Grove, where my sister Kate co-
shared a flat with various friends and which was her answer to
Euston station, there were so many comings and goings. The
man who owned the flat in Lancaster Square was called Rutter
and he was always most pleasant and helpful.

The morning we were to depart from Heathrow to
Salzburg, we were up ready and I turned on the TV, just
out of idle curiosity. Instead, at 6am, there was a dramatic
news bulletin about how the IRA had bombed the Grand
Hotel in Brighton the night before. It was during the
Conservative Party annual conference and the bomb did
an immense amount of damage and caused some fatalities
and some very serious injuries, but Margaret Thatcher, the
British prime minister, had managed to escape unscathed.
It was one of the most dramatic news events of the 1980s,
and when we eventually arrived in Salzburg and checked into
our most comfortable hotel, the late 19th century Hotel vier
Jahreszeiten, the man on the desk had heard all the news and
was a little astonished to find two people from Ireland booked
in, admittedly with the most peaceful of intentions. It was
great to be back in Salzburg again, a city with a marvellous
topography, a magnificent cathedral, whose bells I still love to

hear, online, and an abundance of museums and cafés. A truly wonderful city and the Austrians are always so forthcoming with their hospitality.

We hadn't finished with travelling that year. In late December, we headed off to spend Christmas in Nice, this time in rather more luxury, at the Sofitel. But I found the taps in the bathroom tortuous to use and ended up getting a nasty sprain on my thumb, which seems rather ludicrous when you're just using bathroom taps!It was a little reminiscent of the time in Poznan, Poland, where I also managed to do damage to my thumb. But this time fortunately, it didn't require hospital treatment. We found that going to Nice in December was an ideal time, for the simple reason there are no vast crowds of tourists. Besides that, the weather is usually mild and very pleasant.

From Nice, we took the mountain railway, all the way up to Digne, right up in the foothills of the French Alps. It's called the Train des Pignes, because in the old days, the locos were fired with pine cones. These days, the train has been much modernised, but in those days, it was a bumpy old ride in very uncomfortable carriages. At the old station in Nice, since replaced by a characterless modern one, we stocked up with baguettes and a grande bouteille of red wine, which made for a nice picnic on board as we climbed higher and higher into the mountains. In Digne, we found an excellent hotel, but after Sunday lunch, because of the wine and the altitude of Digne, just over 600 metres above sea level, we had to take a rest. We had been lucky on our arrival in Digne;Bernadette had left her purse on the train seat, but fortunately, I'd done a double check on where we were sitting to make sure we'd left nothing behind and found it.

After a couple of days in Digne, which is not a particularly interesting town, we set out for our return journey via Paris. We took a very convoluted bus journey through Sisteron, on the Durance river, and various other places in the Alpes de

Haute Provence, including the unfortunately named town of Die, until we reached the town of Valence, on the main rail line from Marseilles through Lyon to Paris. It was a bitterly cold New Year's Eve night as we waited on the platform for the TGV. Earlier that evening, a couple of bombs had gone off in the station at Marseille, and naturally, we were concerned that another one could have been planted on the train. But fortunately, just over two hours later, the train coasted into the Gare de Lyon in Paris. A great rush of people got off the train and we found ourselves having to join a queue for a taxi. We had to wait a full hour for one, but eventually, we reached our destination, the Bourbon Sofitel in the 7th, an hotel that no longer exists. By the time we arrived, it was getting close to midnight, so we switched on the TV to see the New Year festivities. A variety show was being televised and all the dancers were topless-ideal for New Year-but we were so exhausted we couldn't raise an eyebrow!

The next morning after breakfast, when we were astonished to see one of the women in a large party from the Middle East, abslutely stuffing herself with food. She was elegantly dressed and coiffured, but she ate on an industrial scale, as if she had been starved for weeks. It was an incredible spectacle!After breakfast, I went for a wander round the neighbourhood and it was during that walk that I discovered, at the foot of the rue de Bellechasse, right opposite what is now the Musée d'Orsay, the Hotel Bellechasse. These days of course, it's much more primped up, with prices to match, but in those days it was a rather plain and inexpensive hotel, where the staff were very friendly and always made us very welcome. For a number of years afterwards, it became our base whenever we visited Paris.

Then, eventually, as the New Year of 1985 was being ushered in, we flew back to Dublin, where I had an utterly tedious job as a trade magazine editor, the sort of job where you just go through the motions (not that sort!), before I was able to break free in 1989.

1985 France, Switzerland

This was the year that we made three trips to France, but first of all came a journey through southern Switzerland, the Italian speaking part.

The trip started in Lausanne, a return visit to this city we enjoyed so much, set beside Lake Léman, and from there, we took the train alongside the lake, and into the mountains, passing through such towns as Monthey and Sion, until we got to Brig.

Brig was an enchanting place, with some fine mountain walks within near distance to the town. Then came the trip through the 20 km long Simplon tunnel, until recently, the longest railway tunnel in Switzerland. As the journey through the tunnel became increasingly claustrophobic, when we emerged into bright daylight once more, we were highly relieved. On the Italian side of the tunnel, the train stopped at Domodóssola, where we took a small train across the mountains to Lugano. The train was rather primitive but it was an interesting journey, as far as Locarno at the end of the line. Locarno has long been famed for the post-first world war treaties signed there in 1925, but this was our first visit.

Before we had set out on this trip to Switzerland, Bernadette had had a very strange dream, of seeing someone jumping out of a plane, his parachute opening out and then him landing in Lake Maggiore, beside Locarno. The day after we arrived, we were walking in a lakeside park, when suddenly, a low flying plane appeared overhead. As it flew over the lake, a sky diver jumped out, his parachute opened and then he landed in the water. The whole sequence of events was exactly as Bernadette had foreseen them.

From Locarno, we moved on to Lugano, the capital of Italian speaking Switzerland, set on the lake of the same name, where we spent a few days. We found this by far the most agreeable part of Switzerland since it is much softer than the German speaking or even the French speaking part of Switzerland. It is thoroughly Italian in style and culture, yet without that big drawback of everyday life in Italy, gross inefficiency. The hotel we stayed in was comfortable and on the Saturday evening, we decided to make an al fresco dinner that we could eat in the room while Eurovision was on. The annual TV song contest was marginally less tedious then than it is now, but halfway through, I dozed off and missed the rest of it, perhaps the most sensible approach to the whole event.

We also took a trip down to see Lake Como, on a very grey and drizzly Saturday afternoon that wasn't at all conducive to sightseeing. But another fascinating place we stopped off at was Campione, with its casino; it's in a small Italian enclave in the southern Swiss canton of Ticino.

Then in August that year, we spent some time in Paris; despite the heat, it's just about the best time of year to visit the city, since so many French people are still away on holiday. The French are so logical, but it always amazes me that they stick rigidly to the summer vacation schedules in July and August, when the inevitable result is massive tailbacks on the motorways, especially to the south. On certain "crossover" weekends, the traffic chaos is even worse, since the people coming back from holiday meet the people setting out and the end result is even longer traffic jams. To me, the sensible thing would be to stagger the holiday season from May to September and wipe out all those interminable jams, but such a simple solution seems absolute anathema to the French way of life and getting stuck in traffic holdups that stretch for hundreds of kilometres!

But that August, for the first time, we stayed in the Hotel Bellechasse at the foot of the rue Bellechasse. It's an interesting little street that bisects the boulevard St Germain and runs down to the River Seine. At a halfway point in the street, at least 20 metres above the level of the Seine, there's a little plaque that denotes how far the waters reached during the great flood of Paris in 1910. In those days, the Hotel Bellechasse was a modest hotel, a bit ramshackle, but the rooms were comfortable enough and had television, so we could enjoy watching the news. Breakfast was always a bit hit and miss but the staff were so friendly and welcoming that we made light of all that. Directly across the street from the hotel was the old Gare d'Orsay, which had been out of use as a railway station serving the south-west of France, since 1939. By the early-1980s, there were serious plans afoot to turn the disused station into the Musée d'Orsay, with its wonderful collection of Impressionist paintings. I guessed, and correctly so, that after the museum opened in 1986, the Hotel Bellechasse would up the ante considerably, with prices to match, and that's precisely what happened. It's now a four star luxury hotel.

After the museum did open, we did several tours of it, marvelling at the glories of the Impressionist artists. But we've missed some of the scandals of recent years, including one instance in 2014 when a Luxembourg performance artist called Deborah de Robertis went into the museum fully clad, and then stripped off completely, hell bent on showing her vagina to any passing tourists. She wanted to emulate that famous painting in the museum, The Origin of the World. The museum's administration was horrified, but the tourists obviously enjoyed the sight and got their phones working overtime to take countless snaps!

One of the other sights we were able to enjoy that August was one of our favourite churches in Paris, St Clothilde in the seventh. It a marvellous Gothic church and its most famous organist was the composer, César Franck. We've always enjoyed the soaring interiors and the quiet of the church. Another delight of the seventh, which I'm glad to say is still there, is an exquisite Chinese restaurant, the Grenelle de Pekin, in the rue de Grenelle, almost next to the mairie for the seventh. The owners of the restaurant were always most hospitable and kind to us and even though it's so long since we've been in Paris, we still keep in touch.

Outside Paris that August, we went on a delightful trip to Barbizon, so favoured by the painters of a century and more ago, who began the so-called realistic school of painting there. Barbizon itself is a delightful town, set amid a great forest, with many of the houses adorned with flowers.

The following month, we were back in Paris again-you couldn't keep us away in those days!-but after a brief stay there, we took the train down to La Rochelle on the west coast. La Rochelle with its fine harbour guarded by twin towers, has a special significance for me, because of my Huguenot ancestry. Between the 17th century and the early 19th century, many Huguenots, French Protestants, fled France to make new lives in many other countries, including the Netherlands, Switzerland, England, Ireland and America. I can claim some, but not much Huguenot ancestry, something of which I've always been very proud. The Huguenots were very industrious and hard working and in Ireland, were responsible for setting up the banking industry and developing the linen industry. I've always been inspired by their work ethic.

La Rochelle is a very agreeable town and we enjoyed wandering round, especially one night, when there was a huge outdoor fair. Near to La Rochelle is the Ile de Ré, a favourite holiday destination for many French people. When we were there, the bridge that connects the mainland with the island had yet to be built, so we had to do the crossing by ferry, in rather stormy conditions, but from the little we saw of the island, we concluded that it must be a place of great beauty and fine beach and seascapes. We also visited the Ile d'Aix, which has a lot of Napoleonic connections. In 1815, after his defeat in the Battle of Waterloo, Napoleon spent his last few days on French soil here. But the attempt to reach the largest island in this part of France, the Ile d'Oléron, proved impossible because of poor transport links.

The journey back to Paris from La Rochelle was a nightmare, SNCF at its worst. Halfway through the trip, which should have taken about three hours, the engine of the train broke down and we were stuck for hours, in sweltering conditions, with no onboard air conditioning. When we eventually arrived back in Paris, in a state of absolute exhaustion, we'd been on the train for a stifling seven hours.

But not even that could deter us from returning to Paris that November, as I had some work to do there. That particular trip, we also went to Versailles, but strangely enough, traipsing through the gilded and mirror-laden halls of Versailles, once the seat of the French monarchy, left us cold and unmoved.

1986 France

This year, we did one spectacular trip, to the south-west of France. We had been a little concerned beforehand, because the Chernobyl nuclear meltdown had happened at the end of April, less than a couple of months beforehand and radiation levels had been rising across Europe. But in the event, nothing untoward happened, at least in that respect.

We flew from Paris to Perpignan and spent a night there before continuing our journey by train to the small town of Collioure, much nearer the Spanish frontier. In a bar in Perpignan, we had got chatting with a locally-based artist and she most kindly gave us one of her engravings, of a white unicorn, which we still have. We had read a little about the place and were very tempted;it fully lived up to expectations. When we arrived there, we had a long walk from the railway station into the centre of town, where we had booked a room in Collioure's most famed hotel, the Casa Pairal, old and revered for its luxury. But when we inspected the room, we found the masses of greenery round the window very offputting, as it was obviously a haven for insects, so we checked out at high speed and went in search of somewhere else.

The Hotel Méditerranée was on the road down from the station and was a fair enough walk from the town centre, but we were energetic enough in those days!The hotel was modern, built from concrete, and rather devoid of any luxury in the way of furnishings or paintings;the walls inside our own room were bare concrete, but at least the place was functional, was reasonably priced and our room had a small balcony. The room was too basic and claustrophobic to do anything there except sleep, but that wasn't a big hardship. On many other trips to France, we had often made impromptu meals to eat while while we watched the television news, but we couldn't do that this time, no TV in the room. These days, the Hotel Mediterranée is still going strong, but much enhanced in its comforts since 1986.

Collioure itself is a fascinating medieval town that has changed little over the centuries, very influenced by Catalan culture rather than by mainstream French. At the centre of the town is a vast castle, while on the promenade that runs beside the river as it runs into the sea, there are lots of pubs and restaurants, and we often dined in that area. The town first came to prominence in the early 20th century when many renowned artists of the calibre of Braque, Matisse and Picasso, lived and worked there. Some of the artists working there then paid their bills with their paintings rather than in cash, creating some priceless local collections. Ever since then, it has retained its artistic ambience and fortunately, any recent developments have been on the fringes of the town, which is often symbolised by its unique looking church of Nôtre Dame, whose foundations are beside the beach and below sea level. The unique bell tower near the church-the two are the symbols of Collioure-was once a lighthouse.

We enjoyed wandering through all the narrow streets, with their traditional food and wine shops. I thought to myself that if this had been Dublin, the whole place would have overrun by vast office blocks occupied by insurance companies, blocks totally devoid of the slightest architectural merit. Collioure was also home to a distinguished writer, Patrick O'Brian, the author of the famous Aubrey/ Maturin seafaring novels set in Napoleonic times. He and his wife Mary lived in Collioure from 1949 onwards;Mary pre-deceased him and he died in 2000, in an hotel in Dublin. They are buried together in Collioure. For many years, everyone assumed O'Brian was an Irish writer, but he was nothing of the sort, English through and through!I also remember reading in Collioure copies of France-Soir, then a broadsheet packed with news;it became a very irrelevant tabloid before closing in 2011. In its heyday, when it was a very well put together popular newspaper, it sold 1.5 million copies a day.

The place is also renowned for its vineyards and in recent years, red and white wine from the vineyards on the hills surrounding Collioure have become much more widely known. When we were there, they were scarcely known outside the town itself.

It's also renowned for its beaches and it has become a mecca for tourists from other parts of France, yet despite its history and its beauty, it remains something of a mystery outside France. I've only met two other couples in Ireland-they live close to us in Dublin-who've actually been to Collioure and enjoyed it as much as we did.

But the place was nearly our downfall. One sunny afternoon, we went for a walk far beyond the town, as far as a small jetty about three km from the town centre. We saw a boat loading up with scuba divers, all dressed in all enclosing black wetsuits. We asked the skipper if there was any chance we could hitch a ride, since it was such a fine afternoon and he welcomed us aboard. But no sooner had the craft got a couple of kilometres out to sea, without even getting past the great cliffs that stand at the entrance to the bay in Collioure, near

Cap Béar, than all of a sudden, a ferocious storm blew up. Within minutes, the sea got incredibly choppy and the rain was lashing down. The scuba divers were all OK;they were well protected against the wet, all the rain and the waves washing over the gunwales. But we had very light summer gear on and in a flash, we were both soaked to the skin. The boat started rising and falling very violently in the waves and before long, it was being so much tossed about that we feared it was going to turn turtle. If that had happened, our survival chances would have been nil. We could see that even the scuba divers were beginning to look very uneasy.

After endless buffeting, the skipper managed to turn the boat round and return to shore, by which time it was bucking so much we felt violently sick, so much so that we almost gave up caring about our plight.

But in due course, the skipper managed to bring the boat back to the jetty from where we had set out with such high hopes a couple of hours previously. There was a small bar nearby, where we repaired at high speed and ordered two large cognacs, followed swiftly by two more, just to be safe. Then, eventually, we plodded back to the hotel, water oozing out of our sandals. We had no lasting effects from the ordeal, but the even to this day, I can bring back to life in every small detail about a quick cruise out to sea that soon turned to ner tragedy.

We enjoyed the rest of our stay in Collioure and at one of the weekly markets, Bernadette found an excellent pair of jeans. The stallholder was very friendly and let her try them on in the back of his van before she bought them. Overall, we rated Collioure very highly, as the most agreeable seaside town we had visited in France. Over the years, we've been to practically every stretch of coast around France and for us, Collioure is top town, far exceeding all the coastal towns on the Cote d'Azur.

Just to the north of Collioure is a much more standardised beach resort, Argelès-Plage, which held little interest for us, but to to the south of Collioure, we found a couple of far more interesting places. Port-Vendres is very much a working port, but it has great atmosphere, despite the fairly large ships loading and unloading their cargoes there. It was once a very busy port, in the days when France controlled much of North Africa and cargo ships and ferries plied between Port-Vendres and North Africa. One rather elderly lady to whom we got talking invited us back to her house, which overlooked the port area, and very kindly insisted on us having a couple of drinks with her. Later on, when we had got back to Dublin, I was chatting in The Irish Times with Brian Fallon, for many years, the paper's venerable art critic, and he told me all about the time he and his wife had spent their honeymoon there. We went even further south, to Banyuls-sur-Mer, another great wine town. Banyuls wine has a lovely sweet taste to it, very distinctive, so it's very much a dessert wine. Wine experts say that modern vintages are very akin to port.

Yet another journey we did from Collioure was to Carcassonne, where we were very taken with the turreted watch towers and fortifications, mostly dating from the 13th and 14th centuries;the old medieval centre of the town known as La Cité is entirely intact and since it was June when we were there, it wasn't overrun with tourists. All in all, a most enjoyable trip and when we flew back to Paris from Perpignan, the Air France Airbus was almost empty, so I had a very amusing experience, talking in French with one of the stewardesses and telling her about many of the cultural events that were on in Paris that summer, and which she hadn't heard about!

We returned to Paris that November, as I had a writing assignment there. What struck us was the weather, which was beautifully sunny, mild and balmy, like an early autumn day in the south of France rather than a month before Christmas. Indeed, the Christmas we spent in Paris was the worst time weatherwise that we've ever spent in the French capital. The place was also deserted;when we arrived at Roissy, we checked into one of the airport hotels. Out of its 600 rooms, we were the only occupants, but the staff kindly opened up the disco, just for us!But that's digressing;this particular November was wonderful in weather terms and we enjoyed wandering round the seventh. When we were there, we particularly enjoyed the brilliant weather on November 17, which is the feast day of a renowned 13th century Hungarian saint, St Elizabeth.

Ever since then, for us, if we get wonderful weather unexpectedly in the run-up to Christmas, we always think lovingly of St Elizabeth's Day in Paris.

1987 France

This year saw us make two trips to France. The first, in June, started in Paris, then we took the train to Vichy, where the collaborationist government led by Maréchal Petain has been in place during the second world war. Today, there's little physical evidence of that regime, that survived by co-operating with the Nazi invaders, but the stain remains on the town. But Vichy itself is a very pleasant and agreeable town, and it has a far more savoury alternative reputation, as a renowned spa town. Many of the building created a century and more ago as part of the spa facilities have a lovely fin de siecle atmosphere to them.

We enjoyed our stay there, partly because in the hotel where we stayed, our room was so large it was almost like an apartment, and we enjoyed making al fresco breakfasts and dinners that we consumed while watching the breakfast and dinner time news bulletins on television. We also had some memorable meals in Vichy, including in the station restaurant. Walks too in and around Vichy were very pleasant, including the evening walk we used to do on the far side of the railway station. Within about a kilometre, the narrow road was into the countryside and it provided an agreeable place to walk.

I made one interesting discovery while in Vichy;in the public library there, I discovered a lot of material about the man who became a President of France, François Mitterand, incredibly secretive in his lifetime. He came from this part of central France and I found out, long before it became public knowledge, that as a young man during the second world war occupation of France, that he had performed a double role. He had worked as a civil servant for the Vichy regime, whilst at the same time, being an active member of the Resistance, with the code name "Morland".

But the next two places we visited on our trip were far less agreeable. The first was Le Puy, a renowned religious mecca, noted for the chapel perched on top of a vast pinnacle of rock. The town itself was ugly and had little to recommend it;we thankfully made our exit to the railway station, only to find that the next town on our itinerary was even worse, Alès, an old mining town. It was scorching hot and the only place we could find for our evening meal was some frightful fast food restaurant. As for digs, we ended up staying in a vast house, in a terrace of houses near the town centre. The house was in perpetual darkness, as all the curtains were pulled shut because of the intense heat. Our room was comfortable enough, but we were amused by the loo, which was up on a raised dais;as we took turns in sitting on the "throne" we pretended to be king and queen!

Then we discovered a real gem of a place, Cassis, which is just to the east of Marseilles. It's set on a very agreeable looking harbour, packed with many tourist boats, while the town itself is very pleasant, with its quiet squares. We found an excellent hotel close to the harbour and it was a good base from which to set out on our explorations. Leading out from the harbour are Les Calanques, or cliffs, which are truly spectacular, now park of a national part. We saw them briefly from a boat excursion.

One place we visited was Marseilles, only half an hour's train ride from Cassis. As we emerged from the railway station, we stood at the top of the steps and admired the fantastic views of the city. A short while before, we had heard my old friend, Dr John de Courcy Ireland, talk on Seascapes on RTÉ Radio 1 about this very view and when we saw it for ourselves I send him a postcard telling him that it was just as magnificent as he had described.

We walked through the Arab quarter of Marseilles, which felt so alien and hostile that it was like being in North Africa, totally un-French, so when we had completed our short walk there, we felt highly relieved. The walk around the great harbour in Marseilles was far more rewarding and we topped it off with drinks at the luxurious Sofitel beside the harbour. We also spent the afternoon lazing beside the pool in an hotel on the coast road that leads eastwards from Marseilles. Other sights we saw in Marseilles included the famous cathedral. We found it a most interesting city, despite its reputation for gangland violence, which continues unabated to this day. Perhaps our most outstanding memory of Marseilles was lunch;we had found a small, unpretentious restaurant that served delicious lunch. As we were tucking in, a party of about half a dozen people came in for lunch. From their talk, they appeared to be civil servants, and we were amazed as they knocked back bottle after bottle of wine, so that their chatter became ever more uproarious. No doubt in the best traditions of civil servants, they then went back to the office, did a smidgin of work and then retired for the day!I always think that French civil servants must make brilliant decisions in the time between returning from lunch, about 3.30pm and going home for the evening at 5pm!

Another trip we did from Cassis was to the wine town of Bandol. En route, the train went through the station at, where the first ever French film was made in 1896. When cinemagoers saw the resulting film on the screen, with a train hurtling towards the camera, panic ensued. We remembered Bandol for something entirely different. We took a boat trip to the offshore island of, it was so hot that afternoon that by the time we got back to Cassis, I was burned bright red, like a well-done lobster, and spent an evening in agony in our hotel room as Bernadette helped me get the intense sunburn under control.

We thoroughly enjoyed Cassis and were sorry to leave it on the way to our final destination, which nearly was our final destination!We travelled back to Marseilles, where we had an excellent lunch at the airport, before taking the plane to Corsica. This turned out to be an extraordinary week. The hotel we stayed in right in the centre of Ajaccio was very comfortable and we enjoyed watching the evening news on television in our room while eating our evening meal. But the view from the windows of our room was really something. The buildings on the opposite side of the street, the rue Cardinal Fesch, were six or seven storeys high;they were all apartments and people lived their lives with the windows open, or else on their balconies, and with all the noise and the hubbub, it was like watching an Italian opera.

The standard tourist sights in Ajaccio were interesting enough, like Napoléon's birthplace, but as always, it was the little vignettes that remain in memory. One small shop in the same street as our hotel, had a lovely selection of scarves for sale and we went in to get one for Bernadette. When she had decided what she wanted and it had been paid for, the little old lady, draped from head to almost toe in a shawl, came round the counter and gave Bernadette a big hug.

Also in Corsica, we took the famous mountain train that crosses from one side of the island to the other, and after going through a massive tunnel, we got off the train in central Corsica to explore the surroundings. But when it came to getting back to Ajaccio, the reality of train departures bore little resemblance to the timetables and the evening train we had been expected never turned up. By about 10pm that night, we were getting desperate as it looked as if we wouldn't get back to Ajaccio, but we went into a bar by the station and explained our predicament. One of the customers was a local taxi driver, who promptly offered to drive us back to Ajaccio, for a very reasonable charge. It turned out to be a memorable drive;as the taxi negotiated all the twists and turns in the mountain roads, the driver had Jacques Brel music playing, and it made the journey absolutely unforgettable.

But another excursion nearly turned into disaster. It was June 13th., St Anthony's feast day, and we decided to go for the afternoon to go to the far side of the bay from Ajaccio. We duly arrived at a luxury hotel, where we had intended to laze by the pool, but as we walked into the reception area, we heard a commotion, and as we were standing there like a couple of eejity tourists, a gang of four or five men, armed with sub-machine guns, had to run past us to get out the front door. They had just raided the manager's office and forced the staff to open the safe. Since the hotel's guests had all paid by credit card, there were plenty of credit card slips in the safe, but very little money. Just a short while before, a similar raid had happened on the Cote d'Azur, and the bandits, enraged by not finding anything, shot and killed half a dozen people.

It was only later, when we had heard the whole story from the hotel staff, that we realised just how dangerous the episode had been. We were offered free drinks on the house, but for some strange reason, I stuck to a bottle of mineral water!Later that afternoon, we went to the nearly beach, which was deserted, so we went skinny dipping in the sea, which was lovely and warm. But Bernadette managed to lose her wedding ring in the sand and despite endless searching, we never found it.

A couple of days later when we were back in Paris, away from all the banditry and political violence that is so much part of the scene in Corsica, we went to a jewellery shop on the boulevard St Germain and bought a lovely replacement.

Our next trip to France came that October. The day we were due to fly out was the day of the great storm in southern England, October 16, which did an immense amount of damage there and in northern France. Our flight to Paris was cancelled and we had to spend the night in an hotel at Dublin airport. But we eventually arrived in Paris, nearly 24 hours behind schedule. I had work to do at the Michelin tourist headquarters on the avenue Breteuil in the seventh. This was for the first Michelin Green Guide to Ireland, in which I was heavily involved.

Once that editorial work was completed, it was off again, next stop the mustard city of Dijon. The hotel we stayed in was very pokey, but it was comfortable and the food was excellent. So too was the meal in the station restaurant. We also had time to go and see the main town in the Chablis wine growing region.

From Dijon, our next stop was Aix les Bains, an historic lakeside spa town, with lots of atmosphere. A long boat trip on the lake was most enjoyable and so too was walking round the town centre. One day, I headed off to Lausanne;at the time, Berlitz was based there and I was also working on some of their guide books, so the day in Lausanne was making taken up with a working lunch with the editor at the times, Giles Allen. When I arrived at the railway station in Geneva, I was astonished to see the newspaper billboards, proclaiming in huge type "Wall Street crash". Black Monday, when the world's stock markets had crashed, had happened the day before, but in those days, long before iPads or mobiles, we hadn't been following the international news.

On my return to a very peaceful Aix Les Bains that evening, I met up with Bernadette who had enjoyed herself moseying around in my absence.

During that trip, we also made brief trips to Annecy, and saw the enchanting medieval houses that line the canals there, and made an equally brief trip to Grenoble, where we were very impressed by the tram system in the city centre. It was nearly 20 years before similar trams appeared in Dublin, on the Luas system. But just as our trip to Corsica in June had resulted in one disaster, losing Bernadette's wedding ring in the sands of the beach, so too did we have another disaster when we returned home from the October trip to find the front door of our flat swinging open;the whole place had been burgled while we were away and it took the best part of a year to get ourselves sorted out and somewhere else agreeable to live, although of course, the psychological consequences of any burglary last far longer.

1988 France

This year we did just one trip to France and it was certainly spectacular;we flew to Paris on Concorde. A local travel agency in Dublin was promoting a weekend trip to Paris to see the famous Arc de Triomphe horse race at the end of September. The flight from Dublin to Paris was on an Air France Concorde. This caught our attention and despite the cost, around IR£1,000, a lot of money for us then, and despite not having the slightest interest in seeing the horse race, we signed up.

We found the supersonic aircraft very small inside, like being squeezed into a toothpaste tube!The aisle down the centre of the plane was so narrow there was barely room for one moderately proportioned person to walk along it, but we fitted into our seats and prepared for take-off. The only other person we recognised on the plane was a young DJ from RTÉ, Gerry Ryan, complete with pigtail. He was obviously on some freebee;years later, in 2010, he died in tragic circumstances in the flat where he lived in Upper Leeson Street, just around the corner from us in Dublin. After he died, there was an almighty hullabaloo and the papers were filled with news about him for weeks and months to come, but these days, he is all but forgotten, except by those close to him.

When Concorde took off from Dublin airport, the thrust was such that we were pushed right back into our seats, then about five minutes later, we were flying over Shannon, in the west of Ireland. The plane headed far out into the Atlantic, halfway to New York, so that it could get up to its maximum speed and height, about 18 km up, almost twice the height of an ordinary aircraft. An indicator in the cabin had a clear display showing the speed of the plane and we were so far above the earth that all we could see was plenty of cloud and the round horizon of the earth. It was a thrilling experience and we were very sad that after the crash of a Concorde in Roissy on July 25, 2000, the fleets of Concordes owned by British Airways and Air France were grounded for good. We still have the paraphernalia that came with the flight, including a cartoon of the two of us done by the inflight cartoonist.

We arrived in Paris giddy with excitement and the Champagne we'd be served on board. The trip also marked the end of a horrendous period for us; we'd spent an awful three months in an absolutely frightful apartment at the top of Ailesbury Road, the poshest road in Dublin. We had found somewhere much nicer to live, fortunately, and as soon as we got back from the trip, we moved into the new house. In Paris that trip, we'd also found a new hotel, as the Hotel Bellechasse had got very swanky and posh and had become much too expensive. We discovered a wonderful hotel on the quays, the Hotel Quai Voltaire, directly opposite the Louvre. It was a bit basic but comfortable and reasonably priced. It also had an illustrious history as such artistic luminaries as Sibelius, Oscar Wilde and Wagner had stayed there, and the great artist, Pissarro, had stayed there to paint the view across the river, to the Louvre. The manager of the hotel, André Etchenique, was a very decent guy who came from the Basque country right down in the south-west of France.

1989 France

This year again, we made just one trip to France, which was in the grip of celebrating the 200th anniversary of the French Revolution. We stayed in Paris, delighted with our new hotel find, the Quai Voltaire. We made one trip out of Paris, to the town of Provins, and enjoyed walking round its medieval battlements. Provins is 100 km from south-east of Paris, so it was quite a long train trip, but when we got there, the sights of the medieval ramparts and the many buildings from the Middle Ages were quite astonishing. It was once home to numerous Champagne fairs, but those days are long over.

1990 France

We made two trips to France this year, one in March, which took in Senlis, and the other in June, to celebrate our wedding anniversary. On this particular trip, we also travelled to Auxerre, where we spent a couple of nights.

Senlis is a most agreeable medieval town 50 km north of Paris, for many centuries a royal town. These days, the amazing Gothic cathedral is the most outstanding reminder of its medieval past. The town itself is delightful, full of ancient cobbled streets and old houses decorated with flowers.

The second trip, to Auxerre, one of the main towns in Burgundy, was equally rewarding. We stayed in a lovely hotel called the Hotel Le Maxime, right on the banks of the River Yonne. Auxerre is blessed with many medieval buildings, most notably the cathedral and the Abbey of Saint-Germain. It's a very agreeable place but when we were there, the murder in the town of a young English language student, had tainted the place and left many unanswered questions. The naked body of the student, Joanne Parrish, had been recovered from the River Yonne in May, 1990.

1991 France

In 1991, we made two trips to France, the first, in March, to Paris and Moret-sur-Loing, the second in August, to Strasbourg.

With our March trip, we were back staying once again in the Hotel Quai Voltaire, but we also made a side trip to Moret-sur-Loing, some 80 km east of Paris. It's renowned these days as having been the home for many years of an outstanding Impressionist painter, Alfred Sisley (1839-1899). He had been born to rich English parents in Paris and lived all his life in France, but always retaining British citizenship. He died in Moret a few months after the death of his wife Eugénie. In his lifetime, he got comparatively little recognition or reward for his paintings, but these days, he's revered.

On that trip to Paris, we also travelled north to the port city of Rouen on the River Seine, had a magnificent lunch at the fairgrounds, where the waitress was full of banter and saw the cathedral.

As a sidelight on all the usual things we did on all these trips to Paris, I had some fun times at some of the sex shows. I well remember one, in the rue St-Denis, near the city hall, where one of the highlights was a young woman who masterbated on stage in front of the audience, making very realistic sounds. A couple of days later, I happened to bump into her in the street and she was a rather plain looking young woman, plainly dressed. There are many ways to make a living and this was just one rather extreme example.

At this same sex show, I had another amusing experience. I am well used to removing young ladies' knickers, with their complete consent of course, but later on in the course of the show, a young lady who was one of the performers fixed her eye on me and came over to me and asked me to take off her knickers, which I gladly did, to the cheers of the rest of the audience.

In another sex place in Paris, I got into conversation with a young lady, who promptly sat there gesturing to me in the clearest terms that she wanted me to masterbate in front of her, an offer I needless to remark declined. Not all the sex shows are on the northern side of Paris;the rue St André des Arts, in the 6th., has a fine erotic venue, too. On one occasion there, two of the female performers put on a special lesbian show for me, and took great delight in licking each other's most intimate parts, in what seemed much more than mere feigned enjoyment.

That traditional side of entertainment in Paris is, I'm glad to report, is still alive and kicking, part of the age-old joy of Paris!

The other trip we did to France that year was to Strasbourg. We did our usual, spending a little while at the Quai Voltaire, before taking a flight to Strasbourg. This was long before the TGV had been extended to Alsace. The runway at Strasbourg airport was closed for repairs, so the plane touched down at a smaller airfield about 30 km from Strasbourg. In typical French fashion, no-one in Air France had thought to organise coaches to take all the passengers to Strasbourg. All the passengers were standing around like so many sheep, wondering what to do, but not actually doing anything. Bernadette marched over to the Air France personnel, gave out hell in her best French and left them in no doubt that they needed to organise a coach in double quick time. One soon appeared, to the cheers of the crowd on the plane, some of whom promptly dubbed her a modern day Joan of Arc!

Despite the intense heat, we enjoyed Strasbourg. All the bureaucrats and politicians from the European Parliament there were away on vacation, so we were able to book into the excellent Hotel Monopole, right opposite the railway station. At any other time of the year, it would have packed out, but we had it almost to ourselves. We enjoyed its comforts and its excellent breakfasts;on the TV news, we were able to see the release of John McCarthy from his captivity in Lebanon. Happily, he is still working for the BBC. Three months later, the man he shared a cell with in captivity, Terry Waite, was also released.

In Strasbourg, we enjoyed seeing the medieval sights of the Grande Ile and Petite-France, on a boat trip, reflecting on the history of Alsace-Lorraine, which changed ownership so many times in history between France and Germany.

We also thought of a former colleague of Bernadette's in the Department of Foreign Affairs, Tommy Woods, a brilliant linguist and scholar, who often wrote for The Irish Times under the byline of Thucycides. Sadly, he was also profoundly alcoholic and while he was on one of his lonely missions for Ireland to the Council of Europe in Strasbourg, he died in the aptly named Hotel Terminus, right next door to where we were staying, in the Hotel Monopole.

Just round the corner from the hotel was a quite pleasant fast food restaurant, where on a couple of occasions, we befriended a very lively young lad who came from the Middle East. He was always ready to have a little chat with us, until his parents became suspicious of him becoming too friendly with westerners, no matter how honourable their intentions. But on a happier note, we sometime dined at the excellent restaurant in the railway station, where we had great fun flirting, in French, with the very lively and friendly waitress. Another place we dined was the renowned Maison Kammerzell, a noted Strasbourg restaurant in a six storey house in traditional Alsation style, close to the cathedral. The tallest spire at the magnificent cathedral rises 142 metres and on a good day, inspired by wine at lunch, we were able to climb to the top with ease. Not these days!

We enjoyed seeing the traditional flower-decked medieval places in Strasbourg, but overall, Strasbourg struck us as rather run down, reminding us in places of Kilkenny back home in Ireland as it might have looked in the 1950s, dull, dreary and poverty stricken then, although it's an exceptionally lively tourism city these days.

There was plenty more to see in Alsace, including Colmar, which has much medieval architecture similar to Strasbourg and where we had an excellent dinner of local specialities one night at the Hotel Bristol. Molsheim, another medieval town, and Kayserberg, a wine town, provided more delights, but when we got to the ultimate wine town in Alsace, Riquewhir, it was absolutely jam packed with tourists, so many that it was impossible to see the sights of the town properly. It was a classic case of tourists and tourism ruining a place of great historical interest. On our trips round Alsace, we saw some of the legendary storks that perch in their nests atop chimney pots. I also familiarised myself with the work of the legendary Alsatian writer and artist, Hansi (1873-1951), who did so much to record the traditional folklore of the region.

We fared much better in Mulhouse, with two exceptional museums. The Cité de l'Automobile has a vast collection of classic cars, the Schlumpf Collection, hundreds of old cars in tip-top condition assembled by the Schlumpf family, once textile magnates in the area. Even more fascinating was the Cité du Train, the largest train museum in the world, packed with old locos and carriages, including old Wagon Lits carriages, and all utterly fascinating. I still have a couple of old railway tickets from there close by me as I write, just to remind me of a truly remarkable place.

Another fine place we visited as Baden-Baden, the spa town just across the frontier in Germany, a very elegant place whose history has been well preserved. The final stop on this trek through the Alsace region was a visit to the Swiss city of Basle, or Basel in Swiss German, on the Rhine, with France and Germany just a very short hop away. We admired the riverside in the city and had a quick look round before returning to Strasbourg. We had been due to meet my friend

Giles Allen from Berlitz in Lausanne, at the station in Basle, but for various reasons, the meeting never worked out and after that, I lost touch with him.

We flew back to Paris from Strasbourg;the flight was very bumpy because of the very hot weather. Paris, on our return, was even more uncomfortable in the intense heat. And that was how our international trips ended;after that visit to Strasbourg and Alsace, Bernadette and I never did any more foreign trips together. I did two more trips on my own, to Britain. In 1994, I went to Glasgow for the day, to research the Scottish ancestors of the family that owns Weirs, the jewellers in Grafton Street, Dublin. The Mitchell Library was a treasure trove of information and the book on Weirs was duly published. Then in 1996, I went to London for a couple of days to do research for a planned book, which never happened, on the history of the old First National Building Society in Dublin.

That was the last time that I left the shores of Ireland. As one gets older, foreign travel becomes less exciting, less fun-filled than it was in one's younger days, and these days, both of us are quite happy to stay put in Ireland. But all the endless travelling, especially to France, was fun while it lasted and provided a rich store of memories.

Travels in Ireland

Abbeyleix

Abbeyleix has long held a place in our hearts, for one place above all, Morrissey's pub. When we made frequent trips to Cashel, Co Tipperary, to stay in the old Cashel Palace Hotel, the main road led through Abbeyleix, long before the M8 motorway to Cork opened. Morrissey's gave us an excellent excuse for breaking our journey and we loved the old-fashioned and unchanged atmosphere of the pub. With a full glass in one's hand, one could easily imagine sitting in the pub in 1900, not 2000.

The main street of Abbeyleix is broad and handsome, almost the width of a Parisian boulevard, and the town has many fine old buildings, including the Market House, built in 1836 and now an excellent library. Also in Abbeyleix in the old days, we often enjoyed lunch in the old Preston House Hotel on the Main Street, in its way, almost as atmospheric as Morrissey's.

Achill

This wonderful island, the largest off the coast of Ireland, occupies a very special place for me, not just because I did a book of old photographs about the island for Stenlake Publishing back in 2012, but because of two wonderful friendships that flowed from that book, Mary J. Murphy from Caherlistrane in Co Galway and Maria Gillen in Athlone. I was also fortunate to meet John 'twin' McNamara, the doyen of Achill historians, who has been a wonderful help to me. The first time I met John, it was in the Gresham Hotel in Dublin, and we spent hours going over all the photographs for the book. Such is John's encyclopaedic knowledge of the island and its history, that by the time we'd finished, the book had practically written itself.

Achill has a very special history and the island itself has a particular magic. It has been home over the years to many remarkable people, including Eva O'Flaherty, who ran the knitting factory there for many years. Her story has been chronicled by Mary J. Murphy. Emily Weddall also played a pioneering role, helping for instance, to start Scoil Acla, the longest running summer school in Ireland. Her life and times are being documented in great detail by Maria Gillen. The introduction to Achill, when you cross the bridge from the mainland, is through the settlement of Achill Sound, not particularly prepossessing. I always remember that one time in depths of winter, when we stayed in the main hotel there, the heating hadn't been turned on and while the welcome was warm in one sense, but in another, it was decidedly chilly!But once you explore the island, especially its coastal areas, it's a different story altogether. On the northern side of the island, there's the deserted village on the slopes of Slievemore, there are the great beaches and the monumental cliffs, culminating in Dooega Head. Not too far away is the modern wonder, Achillhenge, that has survived so many attempts at demolition. It was built from concrete slabs at the end of 2011 and so far, has defied all official attempts to demolish it. At the most westerly point of Achill, Achill Head is a wonderful landscape, but fortunately, it can only be accessed on foot. Elsewhere on the island, however, the developers have been at work and one of the most recent historic places to bite the dust was the Amethyst Hotel, it was once home to the painter that most people connect with Achill, Paul Henry. But despite the developers' depredations, there are still enough places on Achill that remain totally deserted, a wonderful relief from the madding world.

Adare

Bernadette first discovered Adare in the early 1950s, when she spent several holidays there. In those days, it was still a remote country village, renowned for its thatched cottages, built in the 1820s by Lord Dunraven, who owned the big house, now the centrepiece of a golf course. Some of those thatched cottages are still there, reduced in number to nine by a fire in June, 2015, which destroyed two of them.

Adare was where I launched my Mercier Press book in 2010 on Bygone Limerick. The book, which covers Limerick city and county in bygone days, with plenty of old photographs, was a delight to do, most interesting to research and write. We had just the place to launch it, George Stacpoole's antiques shop in the Main Street of Adare, which was absolutely packed for the evening. George, one of the great characters of the antiques' trade, is married to an Italian lady, Michelina, renowned for her fashions. The night of the launch, I stayed in the Dunraven Arms Hotel, where I was very well looked after. Of all the country hotels I know throughout Ireland, I would put this one very close to the top, in terms of historic interest and standards of comfort.

The village has lots of other points of interest, such as the Trinitarian Priory, right next door to the modern heritage centre. But Adare is bugged by two big problems that are taking a ridiculous number of years to sort out, the intense traffic congestion along the Main Street, and parking.

Annalong

In the very early 1970s, before we were married, Bernadette and I spent a weekend in Annalong, on the Co Down coast, travelling there by Ulsterbus from Belfast. We rented a large detached house for the weekend, for next to nothing, and when we arrived, we found there was so much space, we hardly knew what to do with it all. But it was comfortable enough. We enjoyed wandering along the Main Street and venturing down to the harbour, as well as seeing the old cornmill by the harbour;the building has now been excellently restored as a museum. But on the Sunday morning, one small incident occurred, that was intensely irritating then, but which we can now look back on with some amusement. One small shop had been open that morning, in the best North of Ireland tradition of opening as little as possible on the Sabbath. We went to the shop in the hope of stocking up with victuals for lunch and dinner on that day, but it was just midday and the shopkeeper, determined to be as unhelpful as he could, told us in no uncertain terms that he was closing for the rest of the day. We explained our plight;in any part of the southern part of Ireland, a similar shopkeeper would have gone out of his or her way to help, but not in Annalong. The miserable git of a shopkeeper was determined to uphold the Ulster Sabbath at all costs and pulled down the blind on the door and turned the key in the lock.

Antrim

Antrim is a pleasant enough town with a largish population of 20,000, set on Six Mile Water, close to Lough Neagh. It's also an ordinary enough looking town, but we found somewhere of intense interest. On January 19, 1863, Alexander Irvine was born. His mother Anna was Catholic and his father, an unemployed shoemaker, was Jamie, a Protestant. They had married in the days when mixed marriages between Catholics and Protestants were almost totally verboten, ridiculously a sin of the first order. Young Alexander went on to become a minister and one who preached socialist Christianity, very unusual to say the least. He was also very gifted as a writer and in 1913, wrote a book called My Lady of the Chimney Corner, a tribute to his mother. It became a tremendous best seller and made the author famous. Alexander died in California, but was buried in his native Antrim, in 1941. With commendable speed, especially in the middle of the second world war, the humble cottage where he had been born, in Pogue's Entry, was purchased to be turned into a museum, absolutely fascinating.

Close to the town are other places of interest like the round tower, one of the most perfect anywhere in Ireland. We also got to know Shane's Castle and its demesne, with its miniature railway;sadly, the railway is long gone. But Antrim had provided to us a perfect example of how a workaday town can hide some amazing historical facts.

Ardagh

This lovely little model village is a mere 10 km from Longford town and the contrast between the two couldn't be greater. Longford is remarkable for St Mel's cathedral, dating from the early 1840s and miraculously restored in its entirety following a devastating fire. Otherwise my main interest in going to Longford over the years has centred around its two newspapers, the Longford Leader and the Longford News. Also in Longford, in the Longford Arms Hotel, I met Jim Reynolds, who was then running the place. Jim was brother of the late Albert Reynolds, a former Taoiseach, who became a good friend of mine. Jim and his wife Anne died within a day of each other, in November, 2016.

But Ardagh is a completely different story. The Fetherstons built Ardagh House in the early 18th century, then in the later 19th century, they had the village built as a literally model village. It's by far the most picturesque place in Co Longford and the heritage centre in the old village school is a mine of information, including on Ardagh's literary connections with Oliver Goldsmith, Maria Edgeworth and Sir Walter Scott.

Ardara

In the 1970s, before Bernadette and I got married, we travelled through west Co Donegal in a hired van one weekend. We stayed at the delightful Nesbitt Arms Hotel in Ardara;the building itself is quite historic, going back to 1838. We also saw much of the tweed industry, for which the town is famous, and that tweed is well documented in the town's heritage centre. Altogether, we found Ardara a pleasant small town with a population of less than 800. On the Sunday morning there, we had an hilarious experience. We were in our van, parked just off the main street, when all of a sudden, an election meeting began to assemble around us. We were parked beside the platform being used for the speakers;we suddenly saw Brian Lenihan, a noted Fianna Fáil politician, getting up to speak. Bernadette knew him well, but she didn't want him to see her in a decrepit looking van with her boyfriend, so we had to keep a very low profile, heads down, until he had finished speaking!

Ardee

Ardee is a small, but agreeable market town in the east of Co Louth and I used to visit it quite often, back in 1970s and 1980s, as it was then a major centre for the baking trade. In those days, the long gone Ardee Bread Company was a major force in the industry. It's a medieval walled town and its fortified medieval castle is the largest building of its kind in Ireland. Ardee and district has many historical sights, including the jumping church, dating from the 14th century, at Kildemock. where a wall was said to have jumped about a metre after someone's burial close by. In recent years, Ardee has been expanded considerably with many commuters coming to live there, so that today, its population has increased substantially to around 5,000.

Ardmore

What a wonderful seaside village! The BBC journalist and writer Fergal Keane, related to the late great John B. Keane from Listowel, has spent many summers there and has described Ardmore as "heaven on earth". I couldn't agree more. We stayed there several times, always in the old Cliff House Hotel, enjoying meals in the spectacular dining room looking out on the bay. That hotel has long since gone, replaced by an ultra modern hotel of the same name, which has enhanced this culinary reputation. There's not a lot to Ardmore beyond its main street and the cliff walk, past the hotel, which goes past the Cliff House Hotel and eventually leads to St Declan's Well. Continue further along this cliff walkway and you'll see the wreck of the Samson, a crane barge that was in tow from Liverpool to Malta in 1987 when a storm caused it to break its tow. It ended up perched underneath its cliff and it's still there today. The uplands above the cliffs are great walking territory and include such interesting places as the old coastguard station. Ardmore is also renowned for its round tower and the ruins of a medieval cathedral, while in the grounds of the present day Church of Ireland, a well-known and much loved writer whom we got to know quite well, Molly Keane, is buried. She died in 1996. Someone else I knew better also had lots of connections with Ardmore, a remarkable woman, who once lived beside us in Ballsbridge, Dublin, Joan, Countess de Freyne.

Arklow

I've always thought of Arklow as a rather grotty place, in comparison with other seaside towns on the east coast, such as Wicklow town. Admittedly, it does have its points, like the 19 arch bridge that leads into the town, the longest such bridge in Ireland, and its connections with the rebellion in 1798. It's also noted for its harbour. When we stayed there in the 1980s, the hotel we lodged in, in the Main Street, was indescribably drab and lacking in facilities-basic wasn't the word!We also visited what was then an embryonic maritime museum, which I'm glad to say has expanded considerably in recent times. Arklow has always been an industrial town as well as a town with a strong shipping tradition-Arklow Shipping-so inevitably, this industrial development has had its effects on the town.

For a time, over 20 years ago, we had a favourite Chinese restaurant in Arklow and it was so good that we'd think nothing of driving down from Dublin for an evening meal. I was also astonished by the honesty of the owner. A few days after one of our outings there, I was walking along the main road as it comes into Bray and I was a bit puzzled because a car stopped and the driver called over to me. It was the owner of the Chinese restaurant in Arklow. He apologised profusely and said that we had been slightly over-charged for our most recent meal and promptly handed me the cash, with a bit added on. I was gobsmacked to say the least!

Armagh

When we lived in Belfast, I visited Armagh a couple of times, admittedly for as brief a time as possible, as it had a bad reputation during the troubles. Thankfully those troubles are long over, so that today, it's a much more agreeable place. It's noted for its two cathedrals, one Catholic, the other Church of Ireland, as well as for its many fine historical buildings in the centre, its spacious mall, reminiscent of the one in Castlebar. It also has the oldest county museum in Ireland and it's noted for its observatory, so these days, it has plenty going for it, including its reputation for being at the heart of Ireland's apple growing district.

Athlone

In recent years, I've got to know Athlone much better, thanks to my friendship with Maria Gillen, who has given me a much better understanding of the town and its history. Its castle, perched beside the River Shannon, became renowned during the sieges of Athlone during the Williamite wars, 1689-1691, while in much more recent times, one of the most noted people produced by the town was John Broderick, who not only owned and ran Broderick's bakery in the town but was a rather waspish, bisexual man who also made a name for himself in the literary world. Athlone is also renowned of course for being the birthplace of John McCormack, the world-renowned singer.

Athlone has other architectural set pieces, including the Church of Saints Peter and Paul and close by, the modern Luan Gallery. The town was also once renowned for being home to the transmitter of Radio Éireann and 'Athlone' became a familiar name on the dial of radio sets for generations of radio listeners. One of the more recent developments in Athlone is the fine shopping centre. At the time it was being developed, I was doing a lot of work for a magazine that was entirely devoted to the new shopping centres springing up across Ireland, before the Celtic Tiger economy crashed and burned in 2008. I got to know John O'Sullivan, the man who developed the shopping centre, very well as he worked ceaselessly over a number of years to get the project completed. He and his family also own the Hodson Bay Hotel, just outside Athlone, which I've visited on several occasions, as well as other hotels. These days, Athlone is well catered for with excellent hotels, including the Radisson.

During recent visits to Athlone, in the company of Maria, I've enjoyed exploring both banks of the Shannon in the town, as well as its fine restaurants and cafés, such as the Left Bank restaurant. Maria was very involved with the Little Museum of Athlone, which sadly didn't last very long. It was a brave community effort, but the finances weren't forthcoming to keep it running. Maria, in recent times, has also introduced me to a delightful friend of hers, Lucky the cat, a rescue cat, who is owned by a friend of Maria's. Lucky is a cat full of character, always playful. So my recent memories of Athlone are of excellent company, excellent meals out there and lots of historical insights into a town which deserves to be much more recognised on the tourist trail.

Athy

Athy is an engaging market town on the banks of the River Barrow in Co Kildare and it's noted for its many historical connections, including the Quakers and Sir Ernest Shackleton, the Antarctic explorer, who is now commemorated with a fine statue in the town. This is a place with a strong sense of history and plenty of fine historical buildings, such as White's Castle, beside the bridge that crosses the Barrow. The heritage centre has much on the town's history, including inevitably, Shackleton. The town also has another indication of how mores and beliefs have changed so much in Ireland in recent decades. When the very modernistic Dominican church was built in 1965, inspired by Vatican II, it symbolised the new approach to religion in Ireland. But by the end of 2015, the last Mass had been said there, the Dominicans had left the town and the striking looking church had been handed over to the county council.

Balbriggan

Balbriggan is the last town in north Co Dublin before Co Meath;before the motorway was built, it was on the main road from Drogheda to Dublin. When we lived in Drogheda and took the bus to Dublin, we passed through Balbriggan many times. It once had a world-famous textile industry, but these days, it's most noted for being home to so many people from outside Ireland, mainly people who've settled in Ireland from eastern Europe. About a third of its 20,000 population comes from outside Ireland.

These days, Balbriggan's harbour is largely empty of boats;once the town had a thriving fishing industry. It has a beach, the far side of the Dublin to Belfast railway line and it also possesses a Martello tower. The most notorious event in Balbriggan's recent history was the sacking of the town by the notorious Black & Tans, on September 20, 1920. Balbriggan has also been noted, since 1935, for its St Vincent de Paul Sunshine Home;for decades, it has been providing holidays to children from deprived areas and backgrounds. My late brother-in-law, Eamonn Williams, in his younger days, was a helper at the home during the summer holidays and he often told stories of young children so deprived of material necessities that they'd stuff their pockets with bread.

Ballina

Set on the banks of a broad river, the Moy, noted for its salmon fishing, Ballina is a handsome town, with many fine historic buildings. Its most outstanding building is St Muredach's cathedral, set on the banks of the Moy. Ballina is also noted for being the birthplace of a former President of Ireland, Mary Robinson. One of its most recent additions is the Jackie Clarke Museum;during his lifetime, Jackie accumulated a vast amount of memorabilia and artefacts and today, these form the basis of this outstanding museum. The only time I've stayed in Ballina was in December, 1992, when I was doing the Paper Tigers series for RTÉ Radio 1. For the episode on the papers in Co Mayo, I came to Ballina to record some material about the Western People newspaper, based in the town, a newspaper that provided national newspapers in Dublin with many star journalists. Ballina has had quite a procession of newspapers since 1840, including the ill-fated Western Journal, published for six years between 1977 and 1983. The only one that's kept going is the Western People, founded in 1883. When I had my one and only stay in Ballina, it was in a hotel that was decidedly bleak in the run up to Christmas and the only entertainment to be had was watching the Toy Show on the Late Late Show on RTÉ One television;once sampled, best forgotten!

Ballycastle

Out of all the seaside towns in the North of Ireland, this counts as my favourite. It's not nearly as easy to reach as towns on the Co Down coast, as it's 90 km from Belfast, but it's definitely worth the journey. It has a lovely setting, dominated by Fair Head, while out to sea is Rathlin Island. Today's Ballycastle has a population of 5,000 and it's a lively, vibrant place, famed for such events as the Oul Lammas Fair. It's a lovely place and feels secluded, cut off almost, from the rest of Northern Ireland. On one occasion that Bernadette and I stayed there, we had a narrow escape of the most basic kind. We were walking along the seafront, above the beach, when all of a sudden, I felt twitches in my bowels. Whatever I'd eaten for lunch hadn't agreed with me and I had to race back through the town to the hotel we were staying in, a distance of about two km, before I got engulfed in you know what, but fortunately, I made the loo in our hotel room at the Marine Hotel, just in time. It was a bizarre incident, but it never put me off Ballycastle!Incidentally, the Marine Hotel has its Marconi bar and bistro, commemorating the pioneering links Marconi had with Ballycastle.

Near Ballycastle, we also visited the Carrick-a-Rede rope bridge, quite a terrifying experience!Nearby, we also observed the majestic ruins of Dunluce Castle, perched on a headland and dating from the 13th century. We certainly found the Ballycastle area packed with history!

Ballycotton

Ballycotton is a small seaside town about 40 km east of Cork city. It has a fine and dramatic setting, in the lee of Ballycotton island, with its lighthouse. It is principally noted for the rescue of the crew of the Daunt lightship in 1936, when the local lifeboat made the most daring and extending rescue during the history of the RNLI lifeboat service in Ireland.

Ballydehob

This is a lovely little village in west Cork, not far from Bantry and at the head of Roaring Water Bay. It's a small place, with about 800 inhabitants;the district round here was once noted for its copper mining, but these days, it's tourism that's all important. The 150 year old pub in the centre of the village has long been an "institution" in its own right;for many years, it was run by the two Levis sisters, Julia and Nell, characters in their own right. Just outside the village is the 12 arch bridge that once carried the Schull and Skibbereen railway;these days, it makes a great walkway. Also just outside the village is the 13th century Kilcoe Castle, painted pink, owned by two renowned actors, Jeremy Irons and his wife Sinead Cusack.

Ballymena

What can you say about Ballymena?For long the home stomping ground of the late Rev Ian Paisley and his Free Presbyterian church, the place has another unenviable distinction as having the third highest rate of legal gun ownership in Northern Ireland. Ballymena had long had a great manufacturing tradition, of tyres and buses, and the town itself has many fine, historic buildings. A mere 10 km away is Slemish Mountain, once reputed to have been the home of St Patrick.

Ballymoney

Smaller than Ballymena, it's a smaller and more agreeable town, population 10,000, with an equally fine selection of historic buildings. In the days, back in the early 1970s, when I was the editor, improbably, of a trade magazine for the grocery trade in Northern Ireland, I used to come to Ballymema quite often, because it had the headquarters of a large grocery wholesaling firm. Ballymoney also once had a rail link to Ballycastle, but that has long faded into history. Close to Ballymoney are the Dark Hedges, the line of trees, planted in the 18th century that led to Gracehill House and which became the King's Road in the Game of Thrones TV series. Storm damage was caused in early 2016 to the trees, but the majestic line of trees is still largely intact.

Banbridge

In the 1980s, I got to know Banbridge well, because of its booze!In those far-off days, I'd quite often drive to Belfast and on my way back to Dublin, I'd park outside a very handy off licence in the main street. It had a great selection at exceptional prices, far better than anything south of the border, so I'd gaily fill up the boot with bottles of wine and then continue my journey to Dublin. Banbridge is a very historic town, named after the bridge built across the River Bann in 1712. The main street is exceptionally steep in parts and to help horse-drawn loads get to the top of the hill, the great Irish railway constructor, William Dargan, built the underpass, which is still there today.

Bandon

Bandon is an interesting and historical market town nearly 30 km south-west of Cork city. These days, its most famous son is Graham Norton, who is very well known as a TV performer in Britain, indeed one of the greatest stars of the box there;he grew up in Bandon and was educated at Bandon Grammar School. One of the old buildings we found the most interesting in the town was St Peter's Church of Ireland, built between 1847 and 1849. But this is not why we remember Bandon so well, rather for an hilarious episode there. Bandon is on the river of the same name. One weekend in the late 1980s, we were invited to a friend's wedding in Courtmacsherry. We got the train from Dublin to Cork, then the bus as far as Bandon. When the bus stopped on Bandon bridge, we got out with all our luggage and hailed a taxi. We loaded up the taxi and Bernadette got in;at that stage, the driver promptly drove off, completely forgetting that there were two passengers rather than one!I stood in the middle of the road, gesticulating at the driver, and hoping that he'd look in his rear view mirror. It took some time for Bernadette to persuade the driver that he had left behind her husband, so eventually, he did a u-turn, collected me and we all had a good laugh at the incident!

Bangor

After we got married in 1972, we lived in Belfast until 1974. But between 1970, when I first met Bernadette, and our wedding, she often came up to Belfast for the weekend. Very often at those weekends, we'd go off somewhere around the North and one of our favourite places was Bangor in north Co Down, where we really enjoyed our Sunday lunches in the Royal Hotel, facing the waterfront. That was all long before the marina was developed, but after lunch, we always enjoyed our walks along the seafront in Bangor, indeed walking around the town itself, before eventually getting the train back to Belfast. Sometimes on the trip to Bangor, we'd stop off in the town of Holywood and go and visit the Ulster Folk & Transport Museum, with its impressive displays of old house styles and transport, particularly its railway section. These railway exhibits had been located in east Belfast before being moved to the museum in Holywood, so we became very familiar with them in both locations.

Bantry

Bantry, an agreeable seaside town, had two points of historical connection that we always found fascinating. William Martin Murphy, the man who created the old Dublin tram system, developed Independent Newspapers and was the employers' leader in the notorious 1913 Dublin lockout, was in fact a native of Bantry. Someone else of note who came from Bantry was Tim Healy, the first governor-general of the Irish Free State. Someone I got to know well, who also came from this immediate area, was a charming old man called Dan Harrington, who died in 2002. He lived in Pembroke Road in Ballsbridge and his wife predeceased him. Dan had spent most of his adult life working in the building trade in England, before returning home to Ireland. He was a big, cheery country man, full of country lore, and I often used to meet him locally, especially in the old Murphy's newsagents in Upper Baggot Street, taken over by Donnybrook Fair in 2004.

But coming back to Bantry itself, it has a very fine square at its heart, but its real joy is a little outside the town, Bantry House with its elaborate gardens. The house dates from the early 18th century and I remember vividly that when I was working on the first Michelin Green Guide to Ireland, in the late 1980s, I made a particular point of visiting Bantry House and seeing its marvels for myself. When we were there, we met up with the then owner, a most charming man, an aristo of the old school, Egerton Chelswell-White. After his mother died, he had come back from the US in 1978 to run the house. He pointed out the many fine tapestries and other artefacts in the house, which always seemed to be perched on a financial knife edge. But Egerton was most hospitable and gave a great insight into the history and the treasures of the house, invaluable for the Michelin guide. He died in 2012.

Belfast

I've known Belfast since I first came to Ireland in 1962, to go to university in Derry, a singularly ill-fated experience. Belfast didn't particularly inspire me then, especially on Sundays, where everything closed for the day. Later on, when Bernadette and I were starting to get to know each other, we became more familiar with the city especially a Chinese restaurant just off Howard Street in the city centre, where the staff got to know us well and looked after us cordially. After we got married, we returned to Belfast to live, in the east of the city, around the Belmont Road area, which was fortunately always peaceful. The troubles were at their height then, so other parts of the city, including the north and the west, remained unknown territory to us. I always remember one night, we went to an opera performance in a theatre out on the Shore Road, on the way to Larne. The opera was fine, but when it ended, it was impossible to get even a taxi back home, so we had to walk the whole way back to east Belfast, the night sky filled with the continuous sound of gunfire, interrupted by loud explosions.

Similarly, we didn't get to know south Belfast very well either, beyond the Wellington Park Hotel and Queen's University. But despite all the general mayhem, we did get to know the city centre quite well. We also became very familiar with the Strandtown and Belmont Road areas, and out along the Upper Newtownards Road. But even though this part of the city was largely peaceful, when the loyalists staged a general strike in 1974 and brought much of the North to a virtual standstill, we decided it was time to move on. I hired a Mini car, we packed our few possessions in that and headed south to Dublin, to begin a new life.

Bettystown

When we were living in Drogheda between 1974 and 1977, on Sunday afternoons, we often did the walk from Drogheda, beside the Boyne, as far as Bettystown. It was the best part of 15 km, so quite a good walk!On the way, we'd stop off at Mornington, go into the old Star of the Sea church there, and also go and enjoy a few drinks in Moran's pub, which has been there since the early 19th century. When we went there, Agnes Moran was still running it and it was still the old-fashioned pub cum grocery shop, a fascinating place, that had changed little over the decades. The pub is now owned by Brendan and Michelle Butterly, but despite all the changes, I'm glad to say that the fine tree in front of the pub is still there.

Birr

When I was starting my work on the first Michelin Green Guide to Ireland, in October, 1987, I started off in Birr, Co Offaly. Getting there provided the wrong kind of excitement; it was the October bank holiday weekend and on that Friday evening, many people were driving down to Cork for the jazz festival. In fact, it was a non-stop traffic jam all the way from Leeson Street bridge in Dublin to the turnoff for Birr!

When we got to Birr, we checked in at the County Arms Hotel, a little way out of the town centre. The hotel itself was very pleasant but at dinner that night, the only other guest in the dining room was a middle aged woman who was full of marital and other kinds of woes, so we ended up as a captive audience until we could make our excuses and depart. The next day, I found all the neo-Georgian houses most delightful and places like Oxmantown Mall and Emmet Square captivating. The vast demesne of Birr Castle, including its lavish gardens, provided some excellent walks and we got to see the famous astronmical telescope built by the third Earl of Rosse in the 1840s.

Something else that stuck in my mind from Birr was the old-fashioned drapers' shop in the town centre, where I went to buy a pair of gloves, because it was so cold. The owner put Bernadette sitting down on an almost antique chair while I was deciding what to buy.

Bray

When Bernadette and I first started doing a line, one place we visited quite often was Bray, to walk along the promenade and along the paths on Bray Head. We also went for a trip on the old chairlift, that ran to the Eagle's Nest on the top of Bray Head. This chairlift had been built in 1950 and it lasted for 20 years. When we did that trip on it, closure was imminent.

Bernadette often regaled me with stories of what Bray was like when she was a child. When her father Hugh worked for the railways, he was based at Bray station for several years. In those days, the Albert Walk by the seafront was full of novelty and other shops. In those days, the idea of going on a holiday outside Ireland was an impossible dream for working people, so places like Bray were the next best thing.

Buncrana

I remember Buncrana vividly from my days in Derry;the seaside town on the eastern shores of Lough Swilly is only just over 20 km from Derry, so a trip there on the old "Swilly" buses was easy enough. In those days, Buncrana was noted for its pubs and other forms of entertainment, as it still is today, but the place I had a closer connection with was Fahan, on the road from Derry to Buncrana. My English professor at university in Derry was Alan Warner, a most charming and helpful man, who was the only person on the lecturing staff who recognised that my real vocation was writing, not studying. He had a fine house at Fahan, close to Inch island, and I was a quite frequent visitor there. I remember vividly on one occasion, at his house, when we were discussing cars, and I told him that in due course, when hopefully I could afford it, I'd love to own a Mercedes. He told me in the nicest possible way not to have such a ridiculous ambition and now, well over 50 years later, I can well see why he should have poured scorn on the idea.

Bundoran

My visits to Bundoran have been thankfully brief;the honkey-tonk seaside atmosphere never appealed to me and the thoughts of having to spend an vacation in one of its innumerable b & bs never turned me on. What did appeal to me, however, was the fine beach at Bundoran, which in recent years has become a surfer's paradise.

Bushmills

I only visited Bushmills once, a small north Co Antrim village with a population of 1,300, and noted almost entirely for its distillery. It got its licence to distill way back in 1608, so it's the oldest working distillery by far in Ireland. Over the years, it has had various owners, but when I went there in the early 1970s to write a feature about it, the place was owned by Irish Distillers. A young man called Richard Burrows, three years younger than myself, was running the place, and he gave me an excellent and informative guided tour. He himself moved on, as his business career ascended the heights, including a long spell in Paris with Pernod Ricard, the long time owners of Irish Distillers. Along the way, he has also managed to fit in plenty of sailing, another of his enthusiasms. The Bushmills distillery has had various changes of ownership in recent years;its current owner is Mexican, a big spirits conglomerate called José Cuervo.

Cahir

We often used to stop over for lunch at the Cahir House Hotel, right in the centre of Cahir. The town itself is noted for its medieval castle, well preserved, while nearby is the Swiss Cottage, a 19th century cottage ornée. Also close to Cahir, on one occasion, we visited the Michelstown Caves, with the very impressive main cave, with its Tower of Babel, standing 10 metres tall. Between Cahir and Mitchelstown, on the old N8 road, the Kilcoran Lodge Hotel was often a pleasant stopping off place. But one sight in Cahir proved short-lived. Going back about 30 years, there were extensive plans to develop a railway museum here, and indeed several old locos were parked at the station for this purpose, but the plan never worked out. Cahir railway museum closed down in 1993.

Carlingford

One of the most attractive seaside towns in Ireland, Carlingford has long been a favourite spot. When I wrote a book for Stenlake Publishing nearly 10 years ago, in 2008, on Carlingford, Omeath and Greenore, I was able to put my local knowledge to work. I was also lucky enough to have had conversations with a remarkable woman who lived in Carlingford for many years, Mrs Hilda Woods, who died in 2010, just three weeks after her 97th birthday. Her memories of the town were crystal clear, going right back to the late 1930s.

Indeed, Carlingford, with King John's Castle, Taaffes Castle (a fortified merchant house), the old Tholsel and Mint, has a very strong sense of its medieval past, despite much recent building. It also has a very fine visitor centre, in the old Anglican Church of the Trinity. Carlingford also has a wonderful setting on the southern shores of Carlingford Lough.

Carlow

I've always thought of Carlow as a rather dull south Midlands town, with little to recommend it beyond its extravagant Catholic cathedral, its Grecian-style court house and its shopping, but for many years, a most remarkable journalist was at the very centre of its life and times. He was Liam D. Bergin, for 50 years, editor of the Carlow Nationalist newspaper, founded in 1883. He became editor in 1944 and died in 1994, aged 81. Liam was a most enlightened and well travelled editor and one time I interviewed him, I was impressed when he told me that he often tuned into French language broadcasts on long wave. Many journalists who went on to prominence on national newspapers in Dublin had their start here, under his watchful eye;one of them is Des Cahill, the sports commentator on RTÉ, who when he was starting out, worked at the paper between 1979 and 1981.

Carndonagh

The small town of Carndonagh, population 2,500, is in the far north of the Inishowen peninsula;it's a very attractive small town and it's just 15 km from Malin Head, the most northernly point on the island of Ireland. Carndonagh was also one of the first towns in Ireland to see its railway closed, way back in 1935.

Carrick-on-Shannon

I note that Michelin says that Carrick-on-Shannon is a town with little of merit apart as a destination point for tourists taking boating holidays on the River Shannon, but that's rather playing down the merits of the place. True, the river does loom large, and in recent years, with multinational finance operations in the town, Carrick-on-Shannon has experienced a boom of sorts. Its present day population is around 4,000.

One point of interest for me in the town has always been the Leitrim Observer, founded back in 1889. Somehow or other, it has always managed to keep going. Yet the Dunne family, who once owned it, were often cautious;in the old days, the paper also had two other purposes, one as toilet paper, the other as a tablecloth and the Dunnes didn't start cutting the paper after it was printed until the early 1960s. I always remember interviewing one of the older Dunnes and how he told me that in the 1920s, when he was going on his travels round his "parish", he always went with a gun in his pocket, useful in case an advertiser wouldn't pay up.

On the various occasions I've over nighted in the town, it's always been at the Bush Hotel on the Main Street. The hotel has been there for over 200 years. Its current managing director, Joe Dolan-no relation of the singer!-was elected president of the Irish Hotels Federation in early 2016. Four years ago, the Dolan family suffered a terrible tragedy, when their 20 year old son, Andrew, who was studying biomedical sciences at NUI Galway, was attacked during a night out in Mullingar. He died from his injuries.

Carrickfergus

When we were living in Belfast, we made one fleeting visit to Carrickfergus, to see over the remarkable 12th century Norman castle that's in a remarkably good state of preservation. The castle is close to the waterfront and the marina. Louis MacNeice, the renowned poet, who spent much of his life working for the BBC in London, spent his formative years in the town, where his father was the then Church of Ireland rector.

Carrickmacross

This town, on the main road from Dublin to Derry, is famed for its lace, and on a couple of occasions, I visited its lace museum for features I was writing. One of the other claims to fame of the town is that Patrick Byrne (1784-1863), who was the last major exponent of the Gaelic harp, and who was the first Irish traditional musician to have been photographed, is buried here. I also have a personal connection with the town;Catherine Martin, whom I know, is the deputy leader of the Green Party and she comes from Carrickmacross, as does her husband, Francis, also a politician and currently deputy mayor of South Dublin County Council.

A short drive from Carrickmacross, 11 km to be precise, is the village of Iniskeen, birthplace of Patrick Kavanagh, one of Ireland's greatest poets in the 20th century. The heritage centre there, in an old church, is devoted to Kavanagh and I found it most rewarding.

Carrick-on-Suir

This riverside town is some 20 km east of Clonmel, and while the latter is a bustling town, Carrick has seen its population fall considerably to its present level of around 6,000, half what it was at the end of the 18th century, when a whole variety of industries were based there. One of the most attractive sights in Carrick is the 1447 bridge over the River Suir. Sean Kelly, the famed Irish racing cyclist, was born here. Halfway between Carrick-on-suir and Clonmel is Slievenamon, Co Tipperary's "magic" mountain, rising to 719 metres.

Castlebellingham

On occasion in the old days, we'd stop off for lunch at Bellingham Castle, long a hotel, at the end of an impressive tree lined drive. It's on the old N1 road between Drogheda and Dundalk and was once noted for its brewery. We also made the very short trip from Castlebellingham to the seaside village of Annagassan, with its fine beach. It's on the River Glyde as it empties into the Irish Sea. Something like 1,500 years ago, Annagassan was as an important a Viking settlement as Dublin.

Castleblayney

Castleblayney, on the road from Dublin to Derry, has quite a reputation as a musical hot spot. In the 1960s, the place had a thriving show band tradition and one of its local exponents, who went on to a national and international career, was Paddy Cole, whom I know quite well, a most agreeable person who now works as a radio presenter and a musician on international cruises. Anna McGoldrick was another native of the town, while someone else from there who was catapulted to fame is Big Tom, who lives in the nearby townland of Oram. Castleblayney is also beside Lough Muckno, the largest lake in Co Monaghan. Someone who came to national prominence, not to say notoriety, came from near Castleblayney, Eoin O'Duffy (1892-1944). He was an early Commissioner in the Garda Síochána and then became notorious as head of the Blueshirts, the far right wing very Catholic organisation that backed Franco in the Spanish civil war.

Castlebar

The county town of Co Mayo, it's noted for the vast green expanse of its Mall and the nearby Country Life Museum, part of the National Museum of Ireland. It's also the place where Michael Davitt founded the Land League in 1879. These days, Castlebar is home to the present Taoiseach, Enda Kenny.

Castlecomer

We enjoyed exploring Castlecomer, when I was working on the Michelin Green Guide to Ireland. A little north of Kilkenny city, it was one of Ireland's two coal mining centres, the other being on the borders of counties Leitrim and Roscommon. Coal was mined in Castlecomer for over 300 years and was only stopped in 1969. When we were there, it was long before the opening of Discovery Park, with its coal mining exhibition. When we visited, it was a case of examining a few relics of coal mining days that had been deposited in some of the local pubs, some of which have since disappeared, so that today, the town only has four pubs left.

Castlegregory

There's not very much to Castlegregory, on the northern side of the Dingle peninsula in Co Kerry, but it's an attractive and windswept spot, at the start of the Maharees, a sandy peninsula that separates Brandon Bay from Tralee Bay. We found the are a great place for walking, while on one occasion, we climbed the nearby Mount Brandon, all of 952 metres high.

Castlerea

With a population of 3,000, this is the second largest town in Co Roscommon and on the odd occasion I've been there, I've always had a pleasant lunch in Tully's Hotel. The town is quite pleasing, but of course, it's best known for its prison. Some remarkable people have come from Castlerea, including Douglas Hyde, the first president of Ireland, born here in 1860 and elected president in 1938. A more recent person of note who comes from the town is John Waters, a well-known newspaper columnist.

Castletownbere

This is a delightful coastal town on the Beara peninsula, population 1,000. it's one of the main fishing towns in Ireland. Just across from its harbour is Bere Island, while nearby was Dunboy Castle;the Puxley family came here in the late 18th century and built a vast mansion close to the ruins of the castle. The mansion was burned down in 1921, at the end of the war of independence. The Puxleys managed the copper mine at Allihies-you can still see substantial ruins of it today-and these days, there's a museum in Allihies devoted to the area's copper mining.

Castletownshend

This delightful village is a mere eight km from Skibbereen. It's noted for its very steep main street, which leads down to the small harbour. When we were there, we enjoyed a meal at Mary Ann's. The pub has been there since 1846 and today, there's a rustic bar, a restaurant and a bar, as well as an art gallery, the Warren Gallery. The village is also noted for its connection with Edith Somerville, who together with her cousin, Violet Ross, wrote the Irish RM series of humorous novels, under the nom de plumes of Somerville and Ross. Edith Somerville died in Castletownshend in 1949, aged 91, and is buried in the graveyard of St Barrahane's church, just off the bottom of the Main Street.

Cavan

An otherwise unremarkable north midlands town, apart from its Catholic cathedral of Saints Patrick and Felim. It's comparatively new, as construction started in 1938. On the few occasions I went to Cavan, it was to visit the Anglo-Celt newspaper. Founded in 1846, for many years, it was owned by the O'Hanlon family and Willie O'Hanlon, whom I knew well, a rather garrulous character, ran it for many years. Willie was always very helpful and charming, but he was one of those people who just didn't know when to stop talking. The paper had another claim to fame; it was one of the first newspapers in

Ireland to install Linotype machine for mechanised hot metal typesetting. Linotypes came to Cavan at the end of the 19th century and one of the compositors there, James Donohoe, worked at the Anglo-Celt from the time the Linotypes were installed until he retired in 1967. By then, he had set 200 million words of text in hot metal, a feat recognised by the Guinness Book of Records.

Clifden

We made our first visit to Clifden in October, 1982, and we fell in love with the place. It was a lovely town then, scarcely changed over many decades. We stayed in an hotel on the Main Street and when we ran the water for a bath, it came out brown, the colour of the peat bogs around the town. We also visited another noted hotel, just outside the town, the Abbeyglen Castle Hotel. We enjoyed moseying round the town, going down to the seashore and out along the Sky Road, where Kate, daughter of the famed actor Peter O'Toole, has long had a house. We saw the spot where Alcock and Brown landed their trans-Atlantic flight in 1919, close to the Marconi wireless station. In Clifden itself, there wasn't an awful lot to do; Millar's tweed shop was about the only interesting shop in the whole place.

But one night in the bar of our hotel, we had an interesting movie experience. The film ET (Extra Terrestial) had just been released, to enormous global acclaim. Someone had made a clandestine copy of the film remarkably soon after its launch and one night in the pub, this copy of the film was shown to a packed house. The film was quite entertaining and we were a little amazed at how a counterfeit copy of it had made its way so quickly to an out-of-the-way town in the far reaches of Connemara!

I've back to Clifden several times since and on every occasion, I've escaped as quickly as possible. What was once a picturesque small town has been so over-developed that any sign of the atmosphere it had back in 1982 has long since vanished. To my mind, it's a horrible place best avoided. All it's short of nowadays are bars where tourists perform sex acts on one another, shades of Magaluf!

Clogher Head

A pleasant spot just north of Drogheda, where the River Boyne empties into the Irish Sea. The area round here is noted for its commercial fishing, while there are also some remarkable beaches.

Clonakilty

One of the most attractive towns in West Cork, we took an instant liking to Clonakilty, but the first time we stayed there was in an hotel in Emmet Square. It was in the middle of a very cold winter and the hotel had no heating on, which made our stay very unpleasant, but that didn't deter us from enjoying the town. These days, in Emmet Square, there's a museum dedicated to Michael Collins, assassinated not far from here in August, 1922. Places in Clonakilty that were going strong in our time there are still doing the same today, including the delightful Súgán restaurant, run by the O'Crowley family for over 30 years now. And Clonakilty still keeps its close connection with black puddings, although they're something neither of us have had the slightest interest in trying. Another development was just getting off the ground when we were there, the Model Village, depicting the old West Cork railway system, which closed down over 30 years ago. Since then, the Model Village has continued to develop.

Clonmel

In the days when we often stayed in Cashel, we often drove over to Clonmel, to enjoy its delights. Indeed, on some occasions, we stayed in Hearn's Hotel, where Charles Bianconi started his horse-drawn carriage service in 1815. When we stayed there, Hearn's was very rough and ready, although it has been much modernised since. But they were always very hospitable. On one occasion we were in Clonmel one Sunday afternoon and particularly wanted to see something on TV. The management knew us well and even though we weren't staying there, gave us the use of a room with TV for the afternoon, free of charge.

Clonmel has lots of historical points, including the West Gate, the old town walls, the old St Mary's church, and the Main Guard, an historic building that remained derelict for many years, but which has now been restored. One of its features now is a model of the town as it was in the 13th century. The county museum in the town is another fine venue. The town was also where the Irish Labour Party came into being, in 1912. Clonmel is of course on the River Suir and in the bad old days, before flood defences were built, we often saw horrendous floods along the quays.

We were very friendly with the family who ran O'Gorman's mens fashions shop in Main Street-the shop is still there today-and usually after a trip to Clonmel, I'd return home with a purchase from there. Someone else I knew from Clonmel was Tommy O'Brien, for years a music presenter on RTÉ Radio 1;he had once been the editor of the Clonmel Nationalist. He and his sister lived just outside the town, together with his vast collection of music records. In much more recent times, someone I was very friendly with in Clonmel was Edith Power, who for long was chief executive of Tipp FM, the local commercial radio station. Ethel began her marketing career by putting Dublin Zoo and Ryanair on the map, and today, she's running her own consultancy, Ethel Power Marketing, based near Clonmel.

Cobh

We first got to know Cobh when we stayed at the Commodore Hotel and that's close on 50 years ago. We enjoyed wandering round Cobh and its waterfront, seeing the amazing St Colman's cathedral, and sussing out the Titanic connections with Cobh, or Queenstown as it was then, in 1912, then the connections with the Lusitania, which sank three years later, in 1915, off the Old Head of Kinsale. Many victims from that ship were brought to Cobh for burial. In much more recent times, many tourist developments on Spike Island, just offshore from Cobh, have turned it into a another "must see" tourist destination in Cork Harbour.

Cork

Over the years, I've made many visits to Cork, often known as the 'real capital of Ireland'. Many of those visits were to the old Examiner offices, just of Patrick Street, while on occasion, I've been to the RTÉ studios in Fr Mathew Street, as well as seeing the wireless museum in the old jail at Sunday's Well. Cork has many points of natural and historical interest, such as UCC, Fitzgerald's Park, The Lough, the English Market, St Finbarre's cathedral and Elizabeth Fort. On one occasion, we stayed at the old Arbutus Lodge Hotel, when it was owned by the Ryan family. In the late 1980s, it was feted as being one of the top gourmet hotels in Ireland, but we had an unpleasant experience there. We came back to our room mid-morning one day to collect something and found that they were in the middle of repainting the room, which stank of paint. All incredibly unprofessional!The hotel closed down nearly 20 years ago, in 2002, although in recent years, I've kept in touch with Declan Ryan, who is now a noted artisan baker in Cork.

One of the hilarious experiences I had in Cork was when I was there researching for my 1983 book on Irish newspaper history. Ted Crosbie lined up a bevy of veterans and retired people from the Examiner and we all had a most vinous lunch. All I can remember afterwards is that I had to pop into a chemists' shop for something to shore me up until I got the train back to Dublin. Another hilarious experience also had an indirect connection with The Examiner in 1992. I was down there to record some radio interviews. I knew that the session was going to be tough and demanding, so the night before, I decided on an early night at the hotel I was staying in. But over dinner there, I met this Cork woman, who to my astonishment, soon suggested a night of drunken and unrelenting passion. A cool head prevailed and I decided to forego the thrills in favour of being on top of my game the following morning.

Courtmacsherry

We were only in Courtmacsherry once, at a wedding at the end of the 1980s. Under the "Bandon" entry, I'vre told about the hilarious incident with the taxi getting to the village. But we made it allright, for our stay in the Courtmasherry hotel, then run by the Adams family. The village population is a mere 250;it's a very agreeable place but once you've done the walk along the waterfront, you'd seen everything there is to see. One interesting recent development in the village has been the reopening of the village shop as a co-operative.

Courtown

Just short distance away from Gorey, which has become a real commuter town, is the pleasant seaside place of Courtown. It too has seen plenty of development in recent year, sbut it remains a pleasant small resort, complete with its harbour, built between 1839 and 1846. Courtown is always a popular place in summer, but I prefer it in the middle of winter, when the holiday crowds have disappeared until next year.

Derry

When I arrived in Derry for the first time, in October, 1962, to become a third (should that be turd?) level student at Magee University College, I thought that city looked a dour, grey, soulless place with few redeeming features. During the next couple of years I spent in Derry, little happened to change my initial impressions. The place was like some long forgotten backwater of Ulster Unionism, left over from the dark days of the 19th century or even earlier. I soon found out that the Unionist minority in the city held all the keys to prosperity and it did its best to ensure that the majority Catholics/Nationalists/Republicans in Derry got as few spoils as possible. It was an absurdly unjust situation that successive British governments had ignored since Northern Ireland had come into being in 1920.

Even the Guildhall in the city centre, the old city walls and Shipquay Street leading up to the Diamond with its war memorial and the old Austin's department store, all looked forbidding and depressing. No wonder the student pubs that I went to on occasion did such good business, as Magee students sought refuge from the manifest social ills of the city. One of my abiding memories of Derry was living in a frightful flat in Orchard Street, where the walls ran wet with water and where my main diet seemed to be cabbage and custard.

In many ways, the decision to site the new University of Ulster in Coleraine rather than in its rightful place, Derry, marked the tipping point when many people in the city were no longer willing to put up with a stale and uncompromising status quo. It was no great surprise to me that when the troubles started in earnest in August, 1969, the initial flashpoint was Derry, although they soon spread to Belfast. It took a good 30 years to extinguish the fires of the troubles, resulting in the Belfast Agreement of 1998. In the past two decades, I've been back to Derry on several occasions and I've been impressed by the way in which the city has liberated itself from a truly debilitating past, when the social divisions were as strong as they were under the old apartheid regime in South Africa. In recent times, I've found Derry a much more joyous and forward looking place, where everyone can enjoy the rights they are due, and the city seems to have released a great spirit of inner creativity, suppressed for so long under the intolerable ancien regime.

Dingle

We've always found Dingle a delightful place to stay, a small seaside town in a beautiful setting on the Dingle peninsula. It's renowned for its Irishness, although a ridiculous dispute blew up in recent years over what to call the place, especially in Irish. It's also renowned for its pubs, its traditional music, its arts and craft shops, and it has some fine historic buildings, including St Mary's Catholic church, built in 1862, and the much more modern Oceanworld aquarium. Dingle got its own distillery in 2012. When we started going to Dingle, in the early 1980s, dolphins were coming into the harbour quite frequently. One in particular arrived and was soon dubbed Fungi. We went out on a boat trip not long after he had arrived, in 1983, and it's amazing that Fungi is still there today.

We've also driven out from Dingle on various occasions, all round the Dingle peninsula, taking in such sights as Slea Head, Kruger Kavanagh's guesthouse and pub at Dunquin and the Louis Mulcahy pottery at Ballyferriter. We've also been intrigued by the mysterious beehive shaped ancient buildings, built in the eighth century near Slea Head, called clochans and by the remarkably intact, stone-built Gallarus oratory, shaped a little like an upturned boat. Apart from the joys and the delights of the Dingle peninsula itself, from its western edge, there are fine views out to the Blasket Islands.

Donaghadee

When we lived in Belfast, one seaside town we always enjoyed going to was Donaghadee, on the north Co Down coast. It has a very fine harbour that in the 19th century was the Northern Irish terminal for ships crossing the North Channel to Scotland, a role later usurped by Larne and Belfast. Just out to sea from Donaghadee are the Copeland Islands, while in Donaghadee itself, there are such historic places as the motte and Grace Neill's pub, which has been going for the past four centuries and in the 18th century hosted Peter the Great of Russia. The pub began in 1611 as the King's Arms and kept that name for 300 years. A woman called Grace Neill ran it for many years;she died in 1918 aged 98 and the pub was renamed in her honour. Reputed to be the most haunted pub in Ireland, it reopened in 2015 after a short closure. Close to Donaghadee is the Ballycopeland windmill, dating from the 18th century and the oldest windmill in the North of Ireland.

Donegal town

Donegal Town is a fine town with great traditions of making tweeds and carpets. It also has a fine 15th century castle, as well as an excellent train museum. The trains in Co Donegal stopped running close on 60 years ago, but the railway heritage centre in the old station in Donegal Town has plenty of artefacts, even an old railway carriage. It's one of two railway heritage sites in south Donegal, the other being the section of track on the old line that once ran to Glenties;these days, you can still take a short trip on a railcar on the Fintown railway.

Close to Donegal Town, just six km away in fact, is the village of Mountcharles, population just under 500. There's little more to the place than the main street, while the shores of Donegal Bay are close at hand. I remember very vividly going to stay there for a couple of days in 1964. It was then a grim run-down village, blighted by poverty. One day I was there, the weekly cattle market was being held in the main street, which was awash with dung from all the cattle. Add to that all the rain that was pouring down and it was indeed a messy sight. But these days, the main street has been completely transformed and is now clean and bright as a new pin.

Drogheda

We came to live in Drogheda in 1974, having got out of Belfast as quickly as we could during the loyalist strike that year. Drogheda turned out to be a good choice. Our first accommodation was in a damp cottage that we rented from the late Tony Mathews at Colpe, on the southern outskirts of Drogheda. Colpe in those days was entirely rural, but these days of course, it's been covered with housing estates. Tony was a journalist, who worked for both the old Evening Press and RTÉ and his sister Anne worked for many years as a journalist with the Drogheda Independent, so we had lots in common. The cottage was primitive, but it did for a year, until we bought a house on the brand new Oaklawns estate just off the North Road. We got a fixed interest mortgage from the old Drogheda Corporation that cost the grand sum of £12 a month. I remember vividly that one day, Tony Mathews came to see our new house;he took one look around the estate and said to us: 'I can't see you sticking this for long'. He was right;after two years commuting to both Dublin and Belfast on what was then a very unreliable service, we decided to sell up and move to Dublin in 1977. The commuter train service in those days between Drogheda and Dublin was so bad that one evening, when I was returning from Dublin, it was pouring with rain and I had to put up my umbrella inside the carriage.

But we enjoyed all the historical sights of Drogheda, including Millmount, and made many friends, including John Callan, then running a delightful crafts shop and restaurant in Narrow West Street. He met up with and married a nurse, Jane, and we still keep in touch with them. But many other people we knew well in Drogheda have all crossed over to the other side, from which there is no return, including Harry Fairtlough, who did so much to create the museum in Drogheda, Mr Campbell and Barney Woods at Drogheda station (where Barney's wife ran the shop), and Tony Mathews, who was a most hospitable and welcoming landlord, who would often have us down to his nearby house in the evenings to see the 9 o'clock news on television.

West Street in Drogheda is only a ghost of what it once was;Peter Lyons bakery in Stockwell Street and its wonderfully old fashioned shop in West Street are long gone. Another favourite shop of ours in West Street is also long gone, Schwers the newsagents. The old Drogheda library, up in Fair Street, at the back of West Street, was another favourite place. Drogheda of course is renowned for its two churches, both named after St Peter. The Catholic one is on West Street and has the head of an Irish martyr, Oliver Plunkett, while the Church of Ireland church is just beyond Fair Street and has an amazing interior.

Dublin

I've known Dublin longer than anywhere else in Ireland, since I made my first trip to the city five years before I started university in Derry at the age of 19. In nearly 60 years, I've seen immense changes in Dublin and not always for the better. The city is immeasurably better off these days, even if many parts in and around the city centre are still blighted by derelict property, while the homeless problem gets ever more acute. But I've known Dublin long enough to have climbed to the top of the old Nelson's Pillar twice;it was blown up in 1966, just before the 50th anniversary commemorations of the Easter Rising.

My earlier times in Dublin largely centred on Trinity College and in terms of where I have always lived in the city, and where my wife Bernadette and I have lived, it's always been on the southside. In this respect, I'm a true southside Dub at heart:I've never had the slightest desire to live on the northside and any time I'm that side of the city and cross the Liffey on my return home, I always heave a small inward sigh of relief. My late father-in-law, Hugh Quinn, was exactly the same;once, many years ago, he and his family found themselves living in the Crescent at Marino on the northside. He couldn't wait to get back to the right side of the river.

In the old days, Dublin city centre was much more interesting and tempting than it is today. Grafton Street has become little more than a hideous collection of multinationally owned shops, like any other main street in any other town or city in the western world. So these days, I keep out of the city centre as much as I can. Much of the city centre is a personal "no go" area, while the cross-city Luas works have turned the place into a vast building site, where work seems to drag on for ever. Fortunately, suburbs on the southside like Ranelagh and Ballsbridge have changed comparatively little, although these days, there's a new hazard. So many of the residential lanes in

Ballsbridge have become building sites, so people are paying vast amounts of money for the pleasure of living in an ongoing construction nightmare. Greed often, but not always, wins out, especially in Ireland!

Dungarvan

I've always enjoyed the "capital" of west Waterford;it's a fine town, with its centre complemented by Abbeyside on the eastern side of Dungarvan. On the several occasions we visited Dungarvan, we always enjoyed walking along the quaysides and the seafront and looking out to the Cunnigar sandbank in the bay. One place we always enjoyed lunch in was Robert A. Merry's restaurant. It's a very old business, having started as a bottling firm in 1868. But it still has great ambiance and I'm glad to say it's still going strong. Recently, it was voted the best gastro pub in Munster for 2016. It's also very handily placed close to the excellent county museum in the old town hall, which has much wonderful material on the past in Co Waterford. One of my old media friends, the late Tom Tobin from Limerick, was born and brought up in Abbeyside. Among his many skills, he was a fine photographer and after he died, his collection of photographs of this part of west Waterford found an excellent home in the museum.

One of Dungarvan's most distinguished sons, perhaps the best, was William Walton, the Nobel prize winning physicist, who was born in Abbeyside in 1903 and who died in 1995. Long connected with Trinity College, Dublin, I never met him, but Bernadette once had that rare distinction.

Dungloe

Dungloe is an attractive town in west Co Donegal, the main town in The Rosses, and the largest town in the Co Donegal

Gaeltacht. It's fairly sizeable with a population of around 4,000. Its local co-op is renowned throughout the north-west. It began in 1906 and today, its main store is in Dungloe itself, with a couple of nearby branches. As it was starting up, one of its founders couldn't pronounce the word 'co-op' and his pronunciation, The Cope, has stuck! The couple of times I was in Dungloe, with Bernadette, in the early 1970s, had nothing to do with the town's Irish language connections, but everything to do with the superb local fishing, when I, very improbably, was editing a fishing magazine in Belfast called the Ulster Angler.

Ennis

The interesting county town of Clare, set on the River Fergus, and full of narrow medieval streets and lanes, has quite a history. In the days, long ago, when Catholics were forbidden under the penal laws, to live in walled towns, many merchants came from Limerick to live in Ennis, because it had no walls. In more recent times, Daniel O'Connell won a great election victory, declared in Ennis in 1828. A century later, another noted political person also came to prominence in Ennis, Eamon de Valera. He was first elected for East Clare in 1917, re-elected the following year, then in 1923, he topped the poll for Clare, going on to represent the constituency for the next 40 years.

Enniscorthy

This is a small but wonderfully historic town in north Wexford, absolutely bursting with history. The rebels were defeated at the battle of Vinegar Hill, just outside the town, on June 21, 1798. Many relics from 1798 and numerous other episodes in local history are in the Wexford County Museum, which is in the early 13th century castle that towers over the town. Enniscorthy also has a much newer 1798 visitor centre.

Another historic building is St Aidan's Catholic cathedral, designed in the neo-Gothic style by Pugin just over 170 years ago. It's just as impressive inside as it is on the exterior. Enniscorthy also has lots of interesting shops, as well as a pottery just outside the town that's been in business for the past 200 years. There are also fine walks along the banks of the River Slaney. Enniscorthy has produced many outstanding people, including Annie Jameson, the mother of Marconi, the wireless pioneer;Eileen Gray, the 20th century contemporary furniture designer who lived and worked in France for most of her adult life and Colm Tóibin, the distinguished writer.

The place that appealed to me most is just outside the town, Carley's Bridge Pottery, which was founded in 1654 by two brothers from Cornwall and which is still going strong, the oldest pottery in Ireland. It's an amazing place to walk round and see how the pots are first created, and are then fired in the ovens.

This part of Co Wexford is the main area in Ireland for growing strawberries and the Strawberry Fair every June in Enniscorthy is a hardy annual.

Fermoy

Fermoy is an interesting town set on both banks of the River Blackwater in north Co Cork;the present design of the town and the layout of its streets was the work of a Scottish entrepreneur called John Anderson, who bought much of the land on which the town is built, in 1791. Fermoy is also noted for its seven arch bridge across the River Blackwater;it was built in 1864 and 1865, and replaced a 17th century bridge and an even earlier ferry across the river. But even in very recent times, Fermoy has suffered from extensive winter flooding. It also used to suffer from horrendous traffic jams, when it was on the old N8 road from Dublin to Cork, before it was replaced by a motorway.

Galway

I've been to Galway many times over the years and admired its many historical features, including the Spanish Arch, Lynch's Castle, the Galway city museum and what's left of the old Claddagh district, heavily rebuilt in the 1930s. Galway is also home to a very garishly designed modern Catholic cathedral that looks as if it would be better off in Disneyland. Also in Galway, I've much enjoyed visiting the small house where Nora Barnacle, James Joyce's wife, grew up. When I stayed over in Galway on my earlier visits, I usually stayed in the very historic Great Southern Hotel in Eyre Square, now known as the Meyrick Hotel.

My most memorable time in Galway came in September, 2012, when Mary J. Murphy asked me to do the Galway launch of her book on Eva O'Flaherty, the woman behind Achill's knitting industry, at Charlie Byrne's famous bookshop, near the Galway quays. It was a great night, that continued in The House Hotel, where I was staying. This was the first time I'd met Mary, along with her late mother, the lovely and charming Bernadette. Also that night I met for the first time Maria Gillen from Athlone, a great friend of Mary's and ever since, Mary and Maria have been great friends of mine, a wonderful joy over the past four years.

Glenarm

During our time in the North, we spent what was possibly the most miserable Sunday afternoon possible in the small seaside town of Glenarm, just north of Larne. Glenarm is a small town, with a harbour, that's in the most southerly of the nine glens of Antrim. The first castle was built here in the 12th century, but the present day castle is rather more recent, having been built in 1636. With all that history, one would imagine the place would be interesting, but the Sunday afternoon we were there, everywhere was closed up in the best traditions of the Ulster Sabbath. The rain was coming down in sheets and all we could do was take shelter in the local church until it stopped and we could make a rapid exit from the town.

Glencolumbkille

I only visited this tiny village on the south-west corner of Co Donegal once, in 1965, when I was writing a feature about the famed Fr James McDyer. Born in 1910 in this part of Donegal, he served as a priest in England during the second world war, then came home to Ireland. He was sent to the parish of Glencolumbkille in 1951 and maintained his relationship with the place until his death in 1987. From his time in England, he had been acutely aware of the many problems facing Irish emigrants and as for Glencolumbkille, he said it had five curses, bad roads, no electricity, no piped water, no jobs and no social amenities. He set about trying to put matters right, encouraging the setting up of a tweed factory and another factory for processing vegetables, which was later used for fish processing. These days, the folk village, which he helped set up to boost tourism, is still seen as a key part of his legacy. I found him an inspiring person to interview, with his recipe for helping downtrodden communities in the West of Ireland revive themselves. I kept up the friendship with him intermittently, and the last time I was talking with him, shortly before he died, he was staying in the Shelbourne Hotel in Dublin, a long way from Glencolumbkille.

Just before he died, in 1984, came another innovation for Glencolumbkille, the setting up of Oideas Gael, which to this day, continues to provide very popular Irish language tuition and cultural courses.

Glengarriff

This charming little seaside village is between Bantry and Castletownbere, on the Beara peninsula in west Cork. One time we were there, we stopped for coffee in the Eccles Hotel, a remarkable building that looked as if it had been dumped in Glengarriff from the American deep south in the 19th century. In fact, it dates from 1833 and is still going strong. Just offshore from the village is Garnish Island, which covers 15 hectares. In the earlier 20th century, extraordinary gardens were created on the island, which also has a Martello tower. The gardens have been marvellously kept ever since and it's a joy to walk round them.

Perhaps the best known person to have lived in Glengarriff in recent times was Maureen O'Hara, the actress who was born in Ranelagh, Dublin, and became a Hollywood legend. in such films as The Quiet Man. She and her husband bought a splendid house in Glengarriff in 1970, but she didn't take up permanent residence there until much later, in 2005, long after her husband had died. Towards the end of her life, she returned to the US and she died in Idaho in 2015. Maureen O'Hara's only daughter, Bronwyn Fitzsimons, was found dead in the family home in Glengarriff in May, 2016.

Gorey

Gorey is an agreeable town on the road south to Wexford; it's an important commercial centre and in recent years, has seen much housing development occupied by commuters who work in Dublin. One of the big attractions of Gorey is that the seaside town of Courtown is a short distance away, as is Marlfield House, just a short distance from Gorey. It's a wonderfully luxurious country house hotel with 16 ha of fine gardens.

Gorumna Island, Co Galway

Gorumna is really three islands clustered together, Lettermullen, Tir an Fhia and Lettermore, off the south Galway coast, a coastline that is incredibly convoluted geographically speaking. It's easy to get to Gorumna, as there is a bridge linking it to the mainland. Even though the island looks so bleak, devoid of many amenities, it has quite a large population, about 1,000. Most of the island is covered in granite outcrops, which makes it very bleak looking. A couple of medieval church ruins are worth looking at, Maumeen Abbey on the western side of the island and Trawbaun church on the south-east of Gorumna.

Graiguenamanagh

This attractive Kilkenny town is set on a broad stretch of the River Barrow, with interesting riverside vistas.

What really draws people to the place is the Cisterican Duiske Abbey, built in the 13th century, but much refurbished in recent times and with a very striking nave. The town has plenty of pubs and restaurants, as well as Duiske Glass and he Cushendale Woollen Mills. It's also noted for its booksellers and has an annual 'Town of Books' festival, which in 2016, was staged in August.

Grange, Co Sligo

Grange is a small village on the main coastal road, the N15, that links south Donegal with Sligo town. A short distance to the north of Grange are Ballyshannon and Bundoran, while a short stretch further south from it is Drumcliff with its Church of Ireland church and graveyard, where W. B. Yeats was reburied in 1948, having died in the south of France nearly 10 years earlier, just before the start of the second world war. Grange also provides another historical footnote;Lola Montez, an exotic 19th century dancer and a mistress of King Ludwig 1 of Bavaria, came from here. She certainly got on in life, although I very much doubt the hierarchy would have approved!

The village also has a spectacular setting, between Ben Bulben and the Atlantic, so it's in a fascinating corner of the north-west. When I was still in Derry, about 1964, and recovering from an illness, I came here, by bus, for a short holiday in a local b & b. These days of course, Grange has another distinction, two villages of the same name, one the ancient one, the other the modern settlement.

Greystones

I haven't been to Greystones for about 10 years now. We used to love going out there, for walks around the old Victorian harbour and along the seafront road, but since all the carry-on started with the planned developments around the harbour area, we've studiously avoided the place. The old harbour has now been replaced with two modern piers and a marina, so the old ramshackle atmosphere of the previous harbour has been totally dispelled. Work resumed last year on some of the apartment developments planned for the area, so this whole corner of Greystones has been totally changed. We also used to love going to the old La Touche hotel in Greystones, but that too has been closed since 2004 and allowed to fall into a state of dereliction. The old Ormonde cinema on the approach to Greystones from Bray closed down in 2007.

In the old days in Greystones, we sometimes went to the excellent Hungry Monk restaurant on the Main Street, while Bernadette often found clothing and shoes that she liked in the old Bel's shop, also on the Main Street. We often paid our respects at the Catholic church of the Holy Rosary, with its Evie Hone windows. These days, it's much easier to get to Greystones by public transport, as the DART now goes that far, but rather sadly, what's in Greystones these days is, in my opinion, much less interesting.

I also remember well the time that I went there years ago, to do a media interview with a renowned Dutch artist, Marten Toonder, who lived in Greystones for many years. He was a comic strip creator, considered to have been the most successful Dutch artist in this genre. He lived in Greystones from 1965 until the early 1990s, just after his wife died and he died in the Netherlands in 2005, aged 93.

Holywood

Holywood is a pleasant dormitory town on the southern shores of Belfast Lough and on the railway line between Belfast and Bangor. Among its historical sights is a Norman motte, but the main reason why tourists come here is the outstanding Ulster Folk & Transport Museum (qv). Holywood is also famous for being the home town of golfer Rory McIlroy, who learned to play golf on the local course.

Howth

Although Howth is officially part of Dublin city, when you're there, it feels like a place well detached from Dublin. The harbour and marina are most impressive and as I've found for myself over the years, the harbour area is excellent for walks.

From the harbour, it's a short crossing to the uninhabited Ireland's Eye island. The channel is quite narrow, but it's deceptive, because the currents can be so strong.

Two places in Howth I've often enjoyed visiting are the transport museum, which is packed with everthing from old bread carts to old buses and trams. You'll also see many reminders of the old Howth tram, that closed down in 1959. Then as you walk up into the square in Howth village, the old Martello tower has been converted into Ye Olde Hurdy Gurdy Radio Museum. It's jam packed with all kinds of memorabilia about radio and it's engrossing. I've often done the walk up from the village, which incidentally has a good selection of pubs and restaurants, as far as Howth Head. You can also go via the cliff walk, but this can be more hazardous.

Inistioge

The small village of Inistioge, in south Kilkenny, on the banks of the River Nore, is, to my mind, one of the most attractive villages anywhere in Ireland. There's a big tree-lined square and walks from there down to the river. Inistioge is also the last resting place of a famed late 18th century/early 19th century poet, Mary Tighe, who died in 1810. Inistioge also has a heritage centre-where doesn't these days?-and somewhere else well worth visiting are the Woodstock gardens and arboretum. The big house that belonged to what was once the local estate, was burned down in 1922. Apart from its links with Mary Tighe, what I found most fascinating about Inistioge was the Armillary Sphere, an early astronomical device to denote the heavens. But it doesn't tell the time by the sun!

Kanturk

Kanturk is a wonderfully atmospheric small market town set on two rivers, the Allua and the Dalua. It has a total of three bridges. The Greenane bridge was built across the Allua in 1745 and has a Latin inscription on its south parapet, while the humpback bridge over the Dalua has various inscriptions on its northern parapet. The third bridge is the Metal Bridge built in 1848, also across the Dalua. The castle ruin in the town was built about 1609 by MacDonagh MacCarthy, as the biggest mansion belonging to an Irish chief. The English Privy Council decided it was far too grand for an Irish subject and ordered MacCarthy to stop the construction work. He was so incensed that he threw away the blue glass tiles meant for the roof, but the ruins of the castle still stand today.

Kells

Kells is a small, attractive market town in Co Meath that is missing its main attraction, the Book of Kells, which was written here in the eighth century;it's been long resident in the old library at Trinity College, Dublin. But in modern day Kells, you can still see the ruins of the old abbey, the round tower, St Columba's Church of Ireland church and the Market Cross.

Kenmare

Kenmare is a delightful small town, where the Roughty River empties into the Kenmare River. The man who was reponsible for laying out the two principal streets and the diminutive town park in 1775 was the first Marquess of Lansdowne. It's worth going to see the lace museum, commemorating a once-important industry here, and the prehistoric stone circle just off Market Street. These days, Kenmare is a real hub for tourists and they are spoiled for choice with hotels and restaurants.

Kilbeggan

There's just one point of interest in the midlands town of Kilbeggan and that's the famous distillery, which dates back to 1757. You can see all the interesting points of the old distillery, such as the mill race, and you can also explore the traditional methods of distilling whiskey. Today of course the name lives on in a famous brand of Irish whiskey.

Killaloe

Killaloe is a small, attractive town on the banks of the River Shannon, full of atmosphere, and separated from Ballina in Co Tipperary on the far bank of the river by a 13 arch bridge. We enjoyed walking round the interior of St Flannan's cathedral, which dates back to the 13th century, and seeing the Ogham stones, which are some of the earliest forms of writing in Ireland. On the far bank of the Shannon, the village of Ballina is noted for its selection of pubs and restaurants, including Goosers, where we once enjoyed an excellent meal. The name of the place is however open to misinterpretation!

The vast expanse of Lough Derg northwards from Killaloe is very impressive. If you drive just over 30 km northwards from Killaloe, you'll come to Tuamgraney, which dates from the 10th century and which is still used by the Church of Ireland, making it the oldest church in Ireland still used for worship. Tuamgraney is also where the distinguished writer Edna O'Brien was born;these days, well into her 80s, she lives in London.

Kilkee

The main attraction in Kilkee is the great sweep of promenade above a wide sandy beach. The Duggerna Rocks protect the entrance to the bay and you can do what we did once at low tide, clamber over them.

Kill

Kill is a pleasant small village just off the old N7 road between Dublin and Naas. It's noted for its two churches, St Brigid's, the Catholic church, and St John's, the Church of Ireland one. Liam O'Flynn, the uileann pipes player of world renown comes from here. There actually isn't very much to do in Kill, but if you cross the N7 and go to Straffan, on the upper reaches of the River Liffey, there's more there. For starters, there's the steam museum, which has a fascinating array of steam driven models. Straffan had a butterfly museum up until August, 2015, when it was moved to Wallaby Woods, near Donadea, also in Co Kildare. If you have the cash to flash, then stop off at the K Club, where the main building and the estate has an amazing history. I wrote a book about the K Club 20 years ago, so I was down there a lot, with all my meals paid for!

Kilkenny

Tourists flock here and it's not hard to see why! It's a city and it's packed with historical buildings, such as St Canice's cathedral and Kilkenny Castle. At the cathedral, we once climbed the wooden steps in the adjoining round tower to emerge 30 metres above ground level with superb views of Kilkenny. Smithwick's brewery ran in the centre of the city from 1710 until a couple of years ago, but visitors can now enjoy its story at the Smithwick's Experience. The brewery existed here from 1710 to 2014. Liquid refreshments can be enjoyed at many hostelries around the city, including my own favourite over the years, Tynan's Bridge House Bar, with a distinctive Victorian façade and plenty of signs of old times inside, despite modernisation, and the old relics include the low wooden ceiling painted red.

Kilkenny is absolutely packed with places to see and enjoy, which we've done ourselves, including the Design Centre, the Black Abbey, Rothe House, the Tholsel and Kyteler's Inn, where Dame Alice Kyteler, a medieval witch, was said to have been born in 1280. The half-timbered building became an inn in 1324.

Killarney

This is a real tourist mecca, especially with the Lakes of Killarney on its doorstep. The most interesting place we found there was Muckross House, on the outskirts, a vast mansion dating back to the 1840s, but also with many craft workshops and traditional farm buildings. The main attraction for visitors is the national park, which embraces the three lakes of Killarney.

Kilmacthomas

Kilmacthomas is a small village, with a steep Main Street, in west Waterford, best known for Flahavan's, the oatmeal makers, and its vast railway viaduct, which has now been converted to a greenway. It's a great walk along the top of the old viaduct.

Kilmallock

Kilmallock in Co Limerick has a wonderful array of medieval buildings, yet somehow the town languishes off many tourist trails. The couple of times I was there I found its old buildings fascinating, including the abbey, the Collegiate church, Blossom's Gate, the last surviving medieval gate, and the old town walls, which are still quite considerable. Near to Kilmallock is Lough Gur, where you can see many relics from the Stone and Bronze Ages, while also near Kilmallock, it's worth visiting Bruree, the small village where Eamon de Valera, the most outstanding Irish political figure of the 20th century, apart from Michael Collins, was brought up as a young boy. Bruree, with its ancient six arch bridge across the River Maigue, is a pleasant village in its own right.

Kilmore Quay

I've always had a great affection for Kilmore Quay; we've stayed there on occasions and once or twice as well I've driven down from Dublin for the day. The main street still has plenty of thatched houses, but sadly, the old lightship that housed a museum in the harbour was scrapped in 2012. Offshore from Kilmore Quay are the two Saltee Islands, the Great and the Little, which together make up Ireland's largest bird sanctuary. It's well worth taking a boat from Kilmore Quay across to the Saltees, but only in calm weather! Eastward from Kilmore Quay is a fascinating windmill, at Tacumshane, built in 1846 and completely restored in the 1950s.

Kilrush

Kilrush, on the northern shores of the Shannon estuary, is noted for its marina and its heritage centre, while it's also worth taking a boat from Cappagh Pier in Kilrush across to Scattery Island, with the ruins of five mediaval churches and a round tower.

Kinsale

Any time we've been to Kinsale, it's always been jam packed with tourists. It's a real gastronomic hotspot, with restaurants galore, and many people come to Kinsale just for the good eating, as well as for the sailing. The Church of Ireland church of St Multose is worth seeing, as is the Kinsale museum, which has all kinds of relics of the town. Patrick O'Brien, the tallest man born in Ireland, who lived in the 18th century, came from Kinsale and the museum has many artefacts. We particularly enjoyed going out of Kinsale for a few kilometres to the tiny seaside village of Summercove and the adjacent Charles Fort. Much as we enjoyed the good living in Kinsale, especially in Acton's hotel, we did have one unpleasant experience near the town when we ran into a motor rally being run on public roads. It was scary stuff indeed have to stand aside from a whole lot of lunatics in hyped up cars racing along.

Kinvara

In south Co Galway, the small village of Kinvara has a population of around 400;its main attraction is Dunguaire Castle, built in the 16th century. The small harbour at the head of Kinvara Bay is most charming and once a year, a festival takes place to commemorate the hookers that once plied between all the small ports around Galway Bay. The Crinniú na mBád festival was revived in 1979 and usually takes place in August, when up to 100 Galway hookers descend on the tiny harbour. I hasten to add that these Galway hookers are wooden boats with large sails, not the other sort, who attend the hookers' annual convention in Ireland at the Galway Races at the end of July!

Larne

When we lived in Belfast, this was one town we studiously avoided, because it had such a reputation for its loyalist paramilitaries. The town does have its attractions, like the museum and arts centre, while in nearby Glenoe, there's a waterfall and lovely walks. Larne is also renowned for the number of churches it has, lots of religion, but how much Christianity?My abiding memory of Larne is when we were on a train there once, to catch the ferry to Stranraer (these days, ferry sailing from Larne are to Cairnryan). The non-corridor train we were on didn't of course have any loos and all of a sudden, I was bursting with a pee. A drastic solution was needed. I found a plastic bag in our luggage, pissed into it, tied it up and with great relish threw it out of the train window.

Laytown

I've always thought that Laytown was the classier end of Bettystown and we always enjoyed walking on the beach there. Since 1868, the beach in Laytown has been home to an annual horse race, which is quite spectacular. Laytown, at the mouth of the River Nanny, has long been a pleasant place to walk, but of course these days, like so many other places around Drogheda, it has been much developed to house commuters working in Dublin, so much of its old character has been lost.

Letterkenny

I've stopped off here on various occasions; it's an interesting enough place that had its origins as a market town in the early 17th century. The cathedral of St Eunan and St Columba is very impressive, both externally and internally. The county museum is excellent and so too is the library service, which I've found very useful on a number of occasions. I've also contributed to the commercial radio station for Donegal based here, Highland Radio. But what has long fascinated me is the well-known photograph of Market Square in Letterkenny, taken during a horse fair in 1928. The place is full of horses, of course, as well as pony-driven traps and a surprising number of cars.

On one occasion, I stopped off in Letterkenny when I was on my way to Dunfanaghy, a small town right in the north of Co Donegal. I stayed in the renowned Arnold's Hotel, an excellent place, run to this day by the Arnold family, who started it in 1922. These days, of course, Dunfanaghy is on the Wild Atlantic Way, one of those tourism ideas that turned out to be exceptionally bountiful. This little town is also close to such beauty spots as Sheephaven Bay.

Limerick

I've always looked kindly on Limerick, especially since the late 1980s, when I was tested as a possible contributor to Michelin. The French company was preparing to publish the first Irish edition of its Green Guide and wanted a freelance contributor to work alongside a staff journalist in researching and writing all the copy. Half-a-dozen journalists and writers were invited to prepare a Michelin-style entry on various locations around the country. My destination was Limerick, so I headed off there to have a close look at its many sights, including St John's castle, the Treaty Stone and many more. I wrote my script and thought no more of it. Rather to my surprise, a couple of months later, I found I'd won the competition and was duly recruited to Michelin.

Subsequently, for a 2010 book I did on the history of Limerick city and county, told with many old photographs, I was able to research this particular local history in even more depth. I was treated with great courtesy by many people in the city and county and given much help with my historical research. Bernadette and I also enjoyed on a number of occasions staying in Castleconnell, which is just north of Limerick city, and right on the banks of the River Shannon.

Lismore

Lismore in west Waterford has always been a favourite place. The castle here, which I've never visited, has long been the summer home of the Dukes of Devonshire and the sixth Duke was responsible for planning much of the present day town, in the early 19th century. Lismore, on the River Blackwater, is full of architectural surprises, both in some of its residential streets, as well as in the Church of Ireland cathedral, St Carthage's. Lismore is also renowned for its literary connections and one star who was born here in 1931 and still lives here, after all her travels around the world, is Dervla Murphy. We also found an excellent place to eat, Eamonn's Place in the town centre, deservedly still going strong.

Listowel

My abiding memory of Listowel is the night that Bernadette and I dropped in to John B. Keane's pub in the centre of the town. John B was a wonderful host for the night;I told him the work I was doing, for the Michelin guide, and once he had established that my literart bona fides were in order, there was no stopping them. He was a very quiet, unassuming man, but he was happy to spend the whole evening chatting away about almost every subject under the sun. John B died in 2002, but I've still fond memories of that night we spent in his company.

There must be something in the air in Listowel that makes it such a writer's paradise. I reckon that over the years, something like 50 writers have had close connections with the town. Another writer from the area with whom I became very friendly with was Seán McCarthy (1923-1990). I got to known him well, in the RTÉ radio studios in Dublin, when we were both contributors to Sunday Miscellany.

Another aspect of Listowel that appeals to me is the array of plasterwork facades on the front of some of the main buildings around the town square;the best known is the Maid of Erin. These facades were all created by Pat McAuliffe (1846-1921), so these are Victorian creations that have lasted for well over a century. One resurrection in the town is always of great interest, the bringing to life of the old Lartigue monorail train that ran from Listowel to Ballybunion.

Loop Head

When we visited Loop Head, around 25 years ago, the place was indeed barren territory, noted for its lighthouse and little else. But since then, it has developed a strong tourism identity, with people coming to see dolphins in the mouth of the Shannon estuary, as well as enjoying the local food delicacies and the unchanging and spectacular cliff scenery.

Louisburgh

Louisburgh is a very small town, with a population of about 800, on the shores of Clew Bay, about 20 km from Westport. The drive out to Louisburgh is more spectacular than the town itself, although its main street-virtually the whole town-is neat and clean. We also visited the desolate spot of Roonah Quay, which has a slipway from where the small ferry departs to Clare Island at the mouth of Clew Bay.

Lisdoonvarna

We've always regarded Lisdoonvarna as bit of a honky tonk town, mainly because of the spectacular music festival that was staged here from 1978 until 1983, the first festival of its kind in Ireland. These days, other festivals like the Electric Picnic one in Stradbally, are de rigeur. Sadly, in 1983, on the occasion of the last music festival in Lisdoonvarna, in 1983, it wall ended in tragedy. A lethal combination of a turning tide and a subterranean river, along with weather factors, combined to overwhelm eight young men, who were accidentally drowned. But even though the music festival has come and gone, the town has long been famous for its matchmaking festival, still as potent an attraction as ever, where young American women come in search of crusty old bachelor farmers from the West of Ireland.

Malahide

Malahide, just north of Dublin, is a pleasant enough seaside town, although these days, it's turned into a relentlessly middle class suburb. Many developments have been made by beside the estuary, including the marina. The Grand Hotel sits majestic at one end of the town, while at the other end is Malahide Castle and gardens, which have been around for ever, since the 12th century in fact. The gardens used to have a fantastic model railway display, the Fry Model Railway, but that has been in storage for over a decade. But now The

Casino, a substantial thatched premises, is being developed to house this railway layout and it's due to open in 2017.

Malin

The small town of Malin is about as far north as you can go in Ireland. It's six km north of Cardonagh andif you travel on a further 13km from Malin, you come to Malin Head. Malin was a planned Protestant settlement complete with a triangular green and it has retained its Protestant virtues of neatness and cleanliness to the present day, ensuring that it has won the Tidy Towns competition twice.

Mallow

Mallow is an interesting enough town in north Cork, but it was once a lot more interesting, in the 18th century, when it was a spa town. But just outside Mallow is a fascinating big house, Longueville House, built in 1720 and run for many years now by the O'Callaghan family. We've stayed there, most comfortably, and dined there as well, beneath the gaze of the portraits of the various Presidents of Ireland. The 200 ha estate that surrounds the house once had vineyards, rare in Ireland, although there's no real reason why Ireland can't join the wine-producing nations of the world. These days, Longueville produces its own apple brandy, as well as its own cider.

Maynooth

Long renowned for its religious training, at the national seminary founded in the late 18th century, Maynooth has also become well-known in more recent years for its university. These days, the religious aspects of Maynooth are much less to the fore of national consciousness, although very recently, the news that some trainee priests were actively seeking gay partners, did create much interest.

Monaghan

When I was preparing my 2014 book on the history of Co Monaghan, I got to know the county town well. I'd often been there before, of course, especially on my way to Derry, but this time, in depth exploration of its fine 19th century architecture and its outstanding county museum, were most rewarding. The historic Westernra Hotel in the centre of Monaghan is a good place to dine, as is the Four Seasons just to the south. You can see the remains of the Ulster Canal in the town;whether the whole length of the canal will ever be reopened, as a tourist attraction, is a very moot question.

Mullingar

We've often been to Mullingar and on various occasions, have stopped at the Greville Arms Hotel, which had close connections with James Joyce. The cathedral of Christ the King in the town is impressive as are Belvedere House and Gardens just outside Mullingar. One particular spot I've always enjoyed going to in Mullingar is Canton Casey's pub, reckoned to be the oldest business in the town, dating back to 1825. My particular connections with Mullingar over the years have been with the Westmeath Examiner. That's the local newspaper where Joe Dolan started work as an apprentice compositor, before going on to create a glittering showbiz career for himself. He is now commemorated by a statue in his home town.

Naas

If you're into massive retail opportunities, in other words, binge shopping, which I'm not, then in and around Naas is your kind of place. Apart from shops, the place doesn't have many other points of interest, apart from the canal harbour. But the reason I got to know it so well was because Bernadette had introduced me to one of her friends from RTÉ, P. P. O'Reilly. He was a consummate broadcaster, born in Liverpool to Irish parents and who had joined Radio Éireann after military service in the Irish Army during the second world war 'emergency'. He worked for the national broadcaster for the best part of 50 years and when the television service started in 1962, he presented many shows, such as Broadsheet, before eventually transferring to radio. For years, he did the review of the newspapers on the 8am and 9am radio news bulletins and it's often said that no-one has ever done it better, partly because he was so particular about his pronunciation.

P. P.'s wife Antoinette was a publican's daughter and she herself became overwhelmed by alcohol for a long time, until she managed to get over it. For many years, the pair of them lived in Bray, but then they moved to the pub on the Main Street in Naas owned by her family. So it was there during the last few years of his life that I met up with P. P. and we would talk endlessly about this, that and the other. The last time I saw him there, just before he died in 1995, his cough was so bad that conversation soon became impossible. A couple of years after his death, I advised Antoinette about her doing a book on P. P.'s time at the microphone and in front of the cameras-it would have been a fascinating glimpse into almost half a century of Irish broadcasting history and all its personalities, but it never came to fruition.

Navan

In the 1980s, I journeyed to Navan quite often, travels encouraged by my friendship with Jack Davis, then the editor of the Meath Chronicle, and his wife Margot, who started a publication called Modern Woman. They were always most hospitable and in 1990 after we had been involved in a bad car crash outside Navan, that was no fault of ours, they were the first to offer assistance to. We'd been driving on the road from Navan to Slane, en route to Drogheda;some eejit coming in the other direction, was driving at speed, weaving in and out of the traffic to overtake. We could see him coming from quite a distance away and then, without warning, he went off course yet again and crashed right into the front of our car. Subsequently, we had to appear at the local court as witnesses when he was charged and convicted. It was a very unpleasant experience altogether, but it didn't put us off Navan, and we enjoyed seeing places there like St Mary's church.

Nenagh

Drive through Nenagh quickly and you'll miss a couple of interesting places. When we were there, we enjoyed the local museum in the old governor's house in the former goal, and the circular keep which is all that remains of the old castle built around 1200. Apart from that, Nenagh had little to detain us.

Newbridge

Newbridge is best known for its vast army presence, which dates back to 1855, in British times. The army and the Curragh have been symbolic of Newbridge ever since the military base was established in 1855. Not too much of interest there, apart from the legion of prostitutes who came from far and wide to pursue a lucrative trade. We also made several trips to the Keadeen Hotel, on the far side of Newbridge. Interestingly enough, Newbridge was the birthplace of two iconclastic figures, Christy Moore, the singer and songwriter, and Clare Daly, the politician.

Newcastle, Co Down

I knew Newcastle well, long before I wrote a book about the place, based on old photographs, for Stenlake Publishing in Scotland. The main point of interest in the town, then and now, has been the splendid Slieve Donard Hotel, but Newcastle has much more to it than that. The promenade is magnificent and at the southern end of the town, the Mountains of Mourne rise up majestically. Hardly surprising, since he wrote such a famous song about them, Percy French, the songwriter and watercolour artist, had a close connection with Newcastle, which is duly honoured. I was greatly helped when I was doing the book by Terence Bowman, who as editor of the Mourne Observer, the local newspaper, was able to fill me in on so much local lore. He joined the paper in 1976, became editor the following decade and retired in 2010 after a distinguished career.

One of the intriguing things I found out about Newcastle was that when the late Seamus Heaney, the world renowned poet, was a student at Queen's University in Belfast, he spent some of his summer vacation time working as a waiter in Newcastle.

Newcastle West

I've always found this town in west Limerick fascinating, partly because of its 12th century castle, which eventually came into Desmond possession, and partly because of the town's long connection, since the late 19th century, with mineral water production. The firm of Nash's has been famous now for the best part of 150 years. Newcastle West can also claim credit as the birthplace of Ballygowan, the mineral water brand that started the whole trade in Irish bottled mineral waters, back in the early 1980s. Newcastle West has another claim to fame as well, this time, poetic, as it was the birthplace of a renowned contemporary Irish poet, Michael Hartnett (1941-1999).

New Ross

I've always enjoyed New Ross, despite it being such a difficult town to navigate in a car. It dates back to the sixth century, but much of the present day town, including its many narrow streets, some incorporating flights of stairs, was built in the 19th century. The town is full of architectural sights, including the Tholsel and the medieval gates. It was in New Ross during his 1963 visit to Ireland that US President John F. Kennedy made his famous speech in which he said that if one of his ancestors hadn't emigrated from the area, today, he could have been working in the local fertiliser factory. Today, one of the town's attractions is the Dunbrody sailing ship moored at its quays. When I was working on the Michelin guide, we stayed at the Old Rectory Hotel, just across the bridge from New Ross that spans the River Barrow. It was a most comfortable hotel, but has long since closed down;subsequently, it was used to house asylum seekers.

From New Ross, we explored the length of the peninsula that leads to the magnificent Hook Head lighthouse, which dates back to the 12th century, making it probably the oldest lighthouse in Europe. We also saw the exterior of Loftus Hall, renowned for the black magic doings inside. One story has it that the devil burst out of the house through the roof, leaving a great hole that could never be repaired.

We also had an amusing incident in the small seaside town of Fethard-on-Sea. It has about 300 inhabitants and it was close to where the Anglo-Normans landed in Ireland in the late 12th century, forever changing the course of Irish history. In much more recent times, the town was notorious for a bitter Catholic/Protestant religious dispute, something which now seems centuries ago, rather than a mere 60 years. We also noted the façade of Jimmy O'Leary's garage, entirely covered in seashells, the original Shell garage perhaps!But the most amusing incident was in the hotel we were staying in. It was basic enough, but it served its purpose. One morning before breakfast, we wanted to make the most of a beautiful morning by going for a quick walk before breakfast. But while one can find oneself locked out of a hotel on occasion late at night, this time round, we were locked in!The hotel had been all locked up for the night and there was no sign of any early morning staff, so we were literally locked in!

Newry

A great friend of mine in the media, the legendary broadcaster Frank Hall, came from Newry and his tales of his youthful derring do there never ceased to amaze me. He also managed to work them into the television series for which he was most famous, Hall's Pictorial Weekly. It was credited with bringing down the 1973-77 coalition government, with its parodies of various ministers, including Richie Ryan, then finance minister. When it came to the 1977 general election, Fianna Fáil made spadefuls of promises, most of which they subsequently had to retreat from, but it got them elected at the expense of the coalition government.

But as for Newry, it's an interesting place to stop off in, including at the innovative town museum. Just outside the town is the famous Egyptian Arch railway bridge on the main Belfast to Dublin line. On one infamous occasion, one Friday night in the mid-1970s, during the troubles, when I was on the train coming back to Dublin, a bomb went off on the track and blew most of the carriages onto their sides. Incredibly, no-one on the train was hurt, but if the bomb had gone off 200 metres down the track, on the Egyptian Arch, it would have been a totally different story.

In the days when I quite often drove to Belfast and back, I often stopped off at the Buttercrane shopping centre and picked up plenty of bargains, especially in wines. For the last few years, the rush of shoppers from South to North has become almost non-existent, but now, it seems like the collapse in the value of sterling is going to cause vast legions of shoppers to head from all parts of the south to shop in Newry and elsewhere in the North.

Newtownards

Newtownards is a pleasant enough town within easy reach of Belfast and while it has various attractions, including the Somme Centre, and Mount Stewart, a magnificent 18th century big house and gardens, nearby, I must admit, we've never visited either. But what we did enjoy doing from time to time when we lived in Belfast, was going out to Newtownards and scramble up to the Scrabo tower. The 38 metre tall structure was built in 1857 to commemoreate Charles Stewart, the 3rd Marquess of Londonderry. It's also a fine lookout point over much of the Ards peninsula.

Passage East

Many's the time we've cross the estuary near Waterford on the car ferry, which runs from Passage East in Co Waterford to Arthurstown in Co Wexford. Both are small fishing villages;Passage East was built in the lee of a big escarpment and it has small squares and streets, as well as three quays. But the real point of interest near Passage East is seeing the site of the Geneva Barracks. It was part of a new town built by the government in 1793 to attract Swiss metalworkers to Ireland, but they stayed no length of time. During the 1798 rebellion, many rebels were held captive in the buildings here and the place became notorious for the many atrocities committed against them.

Portaferry

Portaferry is a delightful seaside village at the far end of the Ards peninsula, where Strangford Lough enters the sea. The town is about 90 per cent Catholic and in recent years, it has become noted for its aquarium. It also has a small car ferry that makes the short journey across the mouth of Strangford Lough to Strangford itself. We had a memorably trip to Portaferry in the early 1970s, when we spent a memorable weekend, before we were married, at the 18th century Portaferry hotel. We certainly stayed in style;our bed was an old-fashioned four poster bed, so we were able to make a few metaphorical notches on the bedpost!Meals there too were most agreeable and the hotel is delightfully situated right on the waterfront.

Later, for something like 25 years, a most hospitable hotelier called John Hurley ran the hotel, with his wife Marie. I originally got to know John when he came to Belfast to manage the newly opened Great Southern Hotel on the Lisburn Road, which only lasted a short time before bombers did their worst. John also spent a time in the 1970s, until 1980, managing the Everglades hotel in Derry, before ending his career in Portaferry. After he retired, after more than 25 years running the Portaferry hotel, he continued to live almost beside it and in his 80s, he died in September, 2016. The hotel itself was closed for a while in recent times, but I'm glad to see that it reopened during 2016, owned and run by a local couple, Cathal and Mary Arthurs.

Portarlington

Portarlington long had a reputation as the most French town in Ireland, although not of course these days. In 1694, Huguenot refugees arrived from France. The town had been built as an English colony nearly 30 years before, but it promptly failed. The hardworking Huguenots, French Protestants, soon made a go of the place. The French church that was built the year of their arrival is still in use today as a Church of Ireland church. But of the 16 French schools that the town once had at the height of its French-style existence, not a trace remains today.

Portlaoise

We've always found Portlaoise, once called Maryborough, a pleasant and engaging town, despite the looming presence of its prison. The town has always been a pleasant place to stop off for a little light shopping or for coffee and these days, it has another claim to distinction. Some 35 per cent of its population are people who have emigrated to Ireland, mostly from eastern Europe, following the accession of many eastern European countries to the EU in 2004.

Portstewart

This is the more sedate of the twin tourist towns on the north Co Antrim coast, rather more refined than its neighbour Portrush. Portstewart, as we found for ourselves, has an agreeable harbour and promenade, with the latter leading to the strand.

Portrush

Portrush, with its sandy beaches and places like Barry's Amusements, is much more like a traditional honky-tonk seaside resort. It has a fine setting, with Ramore Head in the distance, but what has always attracted me to Portrush is the railway station. When it was built in 1855 in mock Tudor style, complete with clock tower, it was one of the most elaborate stations anywhere in Ireland, and certainly outside the main line stations in Belfast, Cork, Dublin, Galway and Limerick, but sadly these days, with just one line in operation for trains to and from Coleraine, it seems much diminished.

Rathnew

Rathnew village itself has little of interest, except for the magnificent Tinakilly Country House hotel, once the home of 19th century shipping pioneer, Robert Halpin. The most recent time I was in Tinakilly, in September, 2016, I was delighted to make good friends with one of the hotel's delightful cats. But it's Hunter's Hotel, close by Rathnew, that's the real magnet. The building began as a blacksmith's forge, before being turned into a coaching inn in the early 18th century. Today, although its has all mod cons, it has a lovely feeling of a time warp, with all its antiques, and its dining room has been little changed, as is the case with its gardens. Talking about gardens, the hotel is a mere five minutes from the equally magnificent Mount Usher Gardens.

Hunter's has been owned and run the the Hunter and the Gelletlie families since 1825 and a formidable hotel lady called Maureen Gelletlie ran the place for the best part of 60 years, until her death in 2010 at the age of 91. She was a wonderful person to have a chat with and any time we were there for lunch, that was one of the highlights, chatting with Maureen.

The Gelletlies, as a matter of interest, have long been known in nearby Wicklow town for their jeweller's shop.

Roscrea

I've always found Roscrea one of the most interesting towns in the south Midlands, with one of its finest points being the three storey 18th century Damer House. It's now well restored, but it's amazing to think that not so long ago, it was nearly demolished as the then local council had the bright idea of pulling it down to make way for a car park. That stupendously brilliant (sic) decision was soon overturned, very fortunately. Roscrea also has the remains of a 13th century castle and an eighth century round tower. During our explorations of Roscrea when I was helping to compile the Michelin Green Guide to Ireland, I also discovered a fascinating collection of old ploughs in the courtyard of the Pathé Hotel. These had all dated from before the mechanisation of farming, which began in Ireland in the 1940s.

Roundwood

Roundwood has long been a favourite place, for one hostelry in particular, the 16th century Roundwood Inn on the Main Street. In the 1950s, when it was a very rudimentary inn, Bernadette stayed there with some of her girl friends during a brief holiday in Co Wicklow but the inn was so damp that she ended up with pleurisy. But for for past few decades, since 1980 in fact, the Roundwood Inn has been in much better hands, Jürgen Schwalm, who hails from an old eastern German territory that is now part of Russia, Kaliningrad, and his Irish wife Áine.

We used to go to the Roundwood Inn a lot for lunch and sometimes, too, for an evening meal, and we always enjoyed the excellent hospitality and food. It was always a great place for meeting celebrities and one person we used to meet quite often there was Garech de Brún. He lives at nearby Luggala and after lunch, we'd sometimes drive up the mountain road and look down on the great valley that contains his magnificent house. Someone else we often enjoyed meeting up with in the Roundwood Inn was the Irish language broadcaster, the late Liam Ó Murchú, who died in 2015.

The village of Roundwood itself has always been a pleasant place to walk, up as far as the church of St Laurence O'Toole. These days, Roundwood has quite a selection of pubs, restaurants and places to stay, as it's an excellent entry point for the Wicklow national park. But one nearby attraction seems set to change, the Vartry reservoir, which has provided much of Dublin's water for the past 150 years. Now it seems, considerable development works are planned for the reservoir.

Skerries

I've long enjoyed going out to Skerries, to walk around the broad main street and along the harbour road. At the end of the harbour road, near the pier, was a fine hotel, The Pierhouse Hotel, now demolished. On occasions, we had a lovely time staying there, enjoying its restaurant and then in the morning waking up to the sights and sounds of the harbour just across the road. Skerries also has another fine attraction, the two windmills, on the road into the town from the railway station. In the town itself, there are fine restaurants and places to stay, such as the Red Bank, as well as the impressive St Patrick's church, next door to the Carnegie library. Skerries Sailing Club is also replete with sailing events and activities and on one occasion, I found writing and broadcasting a script about it for Seascapes on RTÉ Radio 1 most interesting.

But despite all the wonderful sea airs in Skerries, the town is always a place of sadness in our wider family. Bernadette's sister Gloria was married to the late Eamonn Williams and Eamonn's brother was Kevin, who was always full of adventure and at a boat show in the RDS during the mid-1960s, he bought a new boat. He took it out to Skerries, where he lived, and against all advice from local fishermen, who forecast a storm, he took it out to sea with a couple of friends. The storm blew up and sank the boat, with the loss of all crew. Bernadette remembers vividly turning on the 8am radio news the following morning, to hear about the loss of the boat and its crew.

Skibbereen

My main interest in Skibbereen over the years has been its newspaper, the Southern Star. I knew its long term editor and managing director, Liam O'Regan, very well. He was always a most helpful person, but very shy, so when I was in Skibbereen recording for an episode my radio series, Paper Tigers, in 1992, I had great difficulty in persuading him to take part. But in the end, he did. Its one time rival paper, the Skibbereen Eagle, a Protestant paper that was eventually taken over 90 years ago by its Catholic and nationalist rival, the Southern Star, founded in 1889, was renowned for one observation it made, in the late 1890s, and subsequently repeated on various occasions. It noted that it was keeping its eye on the Czar of Russia and the absurdity of a small regional newspaper in Ireland making such a grandiose claim was picked up by the world's media. The claim is still repeated today, much more than 100 years after it was first made.

Liam himself had a remarkable career at the Southern Star, running it with great efficiency and deftness for 50 years, until his death in 2009, at the age of 72. I also remember vividly on one occasion, when I was returning from Skibbereen to Cork, his wife Maeve offered me a lift. She drove often at great speed on what turned out to be a helter-skelter journey, but we arrived safely and in one piece!

Apart from its distinguished newspaper, Skibbereen is a thriving coastal market town, one of the hubs of West Cork. I also found an excellent place to stay, the West Cork Hotel. The town is also noted as well for its remembrance of the horrendous effects the great mid-19th century famine had on this part of the country.

Sligo

The Yeats connections are everything to Sligo, and rightly so. The Yeats Memorial Building and the fine statue of W. B. Yeats outside the Ulster Bank in Stephen Street are but two of the most tangible reminders of the many links the great poet had with this town. Outside the town, of course, that connection continues, in such settings as Lough Gill and the Lake Isle of Innisfree. The town centre of Sligo, on both sides of the River Garavogue, is workaday. Outside Sligo, I've been to such places as the small seaside resort of Strandhill, noted for its 200 year old Dolly's thatched cottage, and for its surfing. The landscape too around Sligo town is most amazing, notably Knocknarea, where the legendary Queen Maeve is supposed to be buried in a cairn on the summit, and the extraordinarily shaped Ben Bulben mountain, north of Sligo.

Spiddal

In 1998, we spent some time at the Connemara Coast Hotel in Furbo, just to the west of Galway city, a pleasant enough place and a good base for touring Connemara. We explored the seaside village of Spiddal, renowned for its coastal setting and its performances of tradition Irish music, Inverin and Rosmuck, going as far as Clifden and Roundstone. The latter village, set on a steep hill above its harbour, has sweeping sea views and of all the places in Connemara, Roundstone is undoubtedly the most picturesque. We also went to see the cottage at Rosmuck once owned by the great Irish patriot Padraig Pearse, but it was closed for renovations. Touring this part of the West of Ireland was a revelation for me, and also for Bernadette, who was revisiting for the first time in 50 years. As a girl, she had spent holidays in Irish speaking households here, where she was able to practice her fluent Irish.

Strabane

Our acquaintance with Strabane has always been fleeting, so say the least, somewhere to pass through on the way to and from Derry. It's set on the River Foyle, is something like 93 per cent Catholic and had many tragic incidents during the 30 years of the troubles. It has also long had an exceptionally high rate of unemployment, so altogether, an unenviable record. But in 2015, the council in Strabane merged with the city council in Derry. On one of the few occasions we stopped in Strabane, it was to have afternoon tea one Sunday in a town centre hotel, an appropriately gloomy and dispiriting place.

Stradbally

We've long found the small village of Stradbally, in Co Laois, not much more than a Main Street, a rather charming place. It's noted for Stradbally Hall, whose magnificent grounds include a miniature railway, complete with a diesel loco from the old Guinness railway in Dublin. A magnificent steam rally is staged here every August, while another notable event here, the Electric Picnic festival, began here in 2004 and continues to this day as one of Ireland's most memorable musical events for younger people. I'm afraid that we're a bit out of the age category that enjoys such festivities!

Sutton

Sutton, a seaside village just north of Dublin, the last stop before Howth, is now part of Dublin city, but it still retains a strong identity. At the crossroads, we've often shopped at what was once the giant Superquinn supermarket, now Super Valu, and dined at the magnificent Marine Hotel, from where there are fine views over Dublin Bay. On the far side of Sutton, heading towards Portmarnock, there are equally fine sea views out towards Ireland's Eye.

But our main reason for coming to Sutton has always been a personal one, for it is here, in St Fintan's cemetery where Bernadette's father, Hugh Quinn, was buried in 1988 and her mother, Mary or May, formerly Tuohy, was buried in 1997. I was exceptionally fond of them and always considered myself lucky to have had two such wonderful in-laws. So on their anniversaries ever since, I've always made the pilgrimage out to St Fintan's cemetery in Sutton, to pay respects to the memories of them. Some very distinguished names in Irish history over the past century are also buried here, including Pádraig Colum, the poet, Ray McAnally, the actor, Micheál MacLiammoir and his partner Hilton Edwards, who made such a contribution to the Dublin theatre, and who are buried together here. Dr Patrick Hillery, a former Irish President, is buried here and so too is the man who was Ireland's most controversial Taoiseach, Charles Haughey. They are all in the new cemetery, but there's an old one, too, and the ancient St Fintan's Well, after which the place is named, is still flowing. Also in Sutton, it's worth visiting the modern church of St Fintan's, which I always do on my visits to Sutton.

Thurles

The main claim to fame of Thurles is that the Gaelic Athletic Association was founded here in 1884, in Hayes Hotel, which we've often visited. There was long a family connection with Thurles that has long fascinated me;the paternal grandfather of Bernadette, was a train driver based here, and her father, Hugh, continued the family tradition by spending all his working life on the railways. Her paternal grandfather succumbed to injuries received in the 1916 Easter Rising, while her maternal grandfather who enlisted during the first world war, was killed on the western front. That's a neat description of the permanent polarities in Irish history. Bernadette's mother traced her roots back to a family rooted in the bacon curing industries of Limerick, the Tuohys.

Tipperary town

This town in Tipperary, now unified as one single county, although it was for long made up of the North Riding and the South Riding, has long been associated with the first world war marching song, It's a Long Way to Tipperary, although these days, it's also noted for the Tipperary Peace Prize, awarded for nearly 30 years now to international figures who've made a difference to peace. In October, 2016, the recipient was John Kerry, the Secretary of State in the American Obama administration. The town itself is interesting enough, while surrounding landscapes, such as the Glen of Aherlow, are magnificent in their natural beauty. In the days when I was still writing business stories, at the start of the 21st century, I became friendly with one enterprising couple, Sarah and Michael Browne, who started a renowned soup company, called appropriately enough, Browne's Soups, deservedly award winning for their excellent taste.

Tralee

The town of Tralee is interesting enough and we've had pleasant stays in the Mount Brandon Hotel. On one occasion there, we had great difficulty in opening the curtains in our room. I eventually succeeded, but not before implanting a footprint on the ceiling close by. How and why I managed to do that remains a mystery to this day!But my main point of interest has long been The Kerryman, for long one of the leading regional newspapers in Ireland. But it's just outside Tralee that the main points of interest lie. When I was researching for the Michelin Green Guide to Ireland, in 1988 and 1989, we visited Blennerville, which is just two kms from Tralee and took great pleasure in climbing to the top of the then newly restored Blennerville windmill.

Years ago, there used to be a railway from Tralee to Dingle and enthusiasts long aimed to restore it. They opened the first section, from Tralee to Blennerville, in 1990, but sadly, it only survived until 2008.

About nine kms from Tralee, to the north, is the magnificent ruin of Ardfert medieval cathedral, while a little further on in the vast stretch of Banna Strand, where Roger Casement attempted to land arms from a German submarine but was captured and subsequently executed by the British. Also close to Tralee is Fenit, the most westerly harbour in Europe, which we've visited on occasion and which is still a working port.

Tramore

The seaside resort of Tramore is one place I've come to know very well over the years. On more recent visits, I've stayed in the Grand Hotel. The hotel dates back to 1795 and it's considered the hotel in Ireland with the longest continuous trading history. The town, which is the largest in Co

Waterford, after Waterford city, has long been known for its amusement park and entertainment activities. But it also has a truly magnificent strand that stretches for five kms;one of the monuments overlooking Tramore Bay is the Metal Man, erected as a warning to shipping, in 1823. The strand is backed by an equally fine promenade, and many's the time I've enjoyed striding the length of it, getting lungfuls of sea air into the bargain.

I also closely associate Tramore with the Walsh family, who've long owned the Munster Express newspaper in Waterford. J. J.'Smokey Joe' Walsh, who was the editor and managing director for many years, until his death in 1992, lived in a magnificent house on Cliff Road in Tramore, where I interviewed him on a number of occasions. From the back garden of his house, the views over the town and the bay were truly magnificent. Smokey Joe's son, Kieran, who took over the running of the paper on his father's death, has also lived in Tramore for many years, with his wife Roswitha and their family.

Tramore was also once noted for a very idiosyncratic railway that ran for the 15 kms or so into Manor Street station in Waterford. For many years, it enabled numerous Waterford families to visit the seaside in Tramore. It started in 1853 and lasted for just over a century, until the accountants at CIE, the state transport company, got their way and had it shut down in 1960. It was a tremendous loss, especially to Tramore, and is still much mourned today. In recent times, I've become very friendly with Frank O'Donoghue, a former chief executive of Waterford Chamber of Commerce, who now writes and produces books. In 2012, he produced a truly magnificent book on the history of the Tramore to Waterford train, 1853-1960, a revelatory example of how a book in this genre should be produced. He followed this up with an equally remarkable book, which he produced with Andy Kelly, on the history of cinema going in the south-east. Frank lives in Tramore with his wife Anna.

If you travel westwards from Tramore, along the narrow coastal road, you pass through such delightful villages as Annestown, Bunmahon, Dunhill and Stradbally. In the 19th century, this part of Waterford was noted for its copper mines and these days, the Copper Coast gives full and due recognition to that mining history.

Trim

If you'll excuse the pun, this is a trim little town in Co Meath, especially noted for its Norman castle, built in the early 13th century, with substantial portions still intact. Other sights include the ruined 14th century tower called the Yellow Steeple. The town is awash with history and in recent years, rather improbably, it has become the headquarters location for the Office of Public Works, which for long was based at St Stephen's Green in Dublin.

Tuam

This small town in north Co Galway is bursting with history and atmosphere, complete with two cathedrals and an enticing Mill museum on the town's past. My main interest in Tuam has long been the Tuam Herald, which goes back a long way, to 1837. It's long been owned and run by the Burke family and still is. For many years, Jarlath Burke was the legendary editor, who died in 1993, aged 76. His son David now runs the paper, which is owned by himself and his first cousin, Iain Burke. Around 40 years ago, when David was a young journalist on the paper and I was in the business of commissioning stories, David provided me with much memorable material from the west of Ireland. We lost contact for many years and it's only within the past four years that I'm happy to say that we've renewed that friendship. The paper is still going strong, one of the few weekly newspapers in Ireland that's still family owned. It also has another claim to fame, the number of distinguished journalists who began their careers there, including the present editor of The Irish Times, Kevin O'Sullivan. He comes from Tramore, Co Waterford and began his journalist career with the Tuam Herald and the Connacht Tribune before joining The Irish Times in 1997. He was appointed editor in 2011.

Tullamore

Tullamore I've always a rather dull place, despite its place on the Grand Canal. But it has one saving feature, its long connection with distilling. The old Tullamore Dew distillery ran from 1829 until the 1950s, and was very famous in its day, "give every man his Dew" and all that. But the Scottish distillery firm of Grants has now revived the tradition. It has invested €35 million in a brand new distillery, opened in 2014. It's all part of the tremendous expansion of whiskey distilling that's been going on in Ireland for the past few years, everywhere from Dublin and Dingle to Midleton, Kilbeggan and the Cooley peninsula. I'll raise a glass to that, since whiskey, the Irish variety, is one of my favourite drinks. Tullamore was also long famous for a rather sweet tasting liqueur called Irish Mist. Not to worry that Irish Mist means something rather different in German-Irish shit!The Wiliams family who owned the old distillery also owned a chain of supermarkets in Ireland called Five Star, long forgotten these days. It was sold to Quinnworth, now Tesco, in 1979.

Warrenpoint

If you're interested in shipping, as I am, Warrenpoint is a good place to be, because it has developed so much in recent decades as a container port. The town itself is best known for its vast central square, but if you've driven a short distance further on, as we have on occasions, the small town of Rostrevor is much more prepossessing. It sits between Carlingford Lough and the Mountains of Mourne and it's full of gracious villas and houses, redolent of a bygone age. It also enjoys remarkably mild weather in winter, so the place is full of palm trees and other species more familiar in sub-tropical climes.

Waterford

Waterford, the oldest developed city in Ireland, its Viking origins well documented, has many fascinating historical aspects, all of which I've explored over the years. They include the old city walls, Reginald's Tower, the People's Park, the Theatre Royal and in recent years, the highly impressive Museum of Treasures. For long, Waterford was home to the Waterford Glass company, but that closed down in 2009, although glass making has been reintroduced, on a smaller scale, in the city centre in recent years.

The city, with its quays, also has a long and honourable shipping tradition;in the 19th century, this was the shipbuilding 'capital' of Ireland.

The city may be awash with history and in more recent times, a veritable blitz of artistic activities, but it still has ghosts from the past. On the heights of Ferrybank, on the far side of the river from the main city, the Ard Rí hotel, opened in the 1960s, was a mecca for functions and events for many years. Indeed, many was the function I covered there. But it eventually closed down and the ruin of the hotel has remained to haunt the city ever since.

But over the years, my closest connection with Waterford has been through the Munster Express. I got to know well J. J. 'Smokey Joe' Walsh, long time editor and managing director, who died in 1992. I got loads of copy about Smokey Joe. The most famous story about him concerned his toupee; it was often said that before he went to a function, he sprinkled salt from a salt cellar, on his shoulders to make it look as if he had dandruff, and therefore, real hair. But the equally legendary John O'Connor, for years news editor at the paper and reviewer of the regional press for RTÉ Radio 1, firmly dismisses this story as being merely the stuff of urban legend, not true at all. I've also been very friendly for many years with one of Smokey Joe's son, Kieran, who took over the running of the paper on his father's demise.

Waterville

Waterville, in the far reaches of Co Kerry, has always been a most delightful place to visit. On occasion, we've stayed at the quite exceptional Butler Arms Hotel, going since 1884 and now run by the fourth generation of the Huggard family in charge. Other personalities, of world renown, liked the place just as much. Charlie Chaplin and his family started coming to the hotel in 1959, for a decade, and today, he is commemorated by a statue in the town. Walt Disney stayed here on occasion and so too did the famous or infamous banker, J. P. Morgan. Just outside Waterville, we enjoyed driving the short distance up into the wilds around Lough Currane. Out to sea, not far from Waterville, are the famed Skellig Islands. A little further on is another rewarding island to visit, Valentia, with its main, but tiny, town, Knightstown, and its great slate quarries.

Westport

Westport has always been a favourite place to visit, it's such an historic town, dating back to the late 18th century. The great Westport House also dates back to then and in recent years, it and the surrounding estate have been developed as a great tourist attraction. But sadly, Jeremy Browne, the 11th Marquess of Altamont, Lord Altamont, died in 2014. He was a great character in his own right, and any time I met him, it was always a case of "do call me Jeremy". The fate of the great house and gardens is to be decided;they were put up for sale earlier in 2016.

Another old place we really loved in Westport was the Olde Railway Hotel, set beside the river, and a most fascinating place to stay and dine. I'm glad to say it has now been restored to its former glory. Westport is renowed for its river and other attractions, such as the Quay area. I've also had many dealings over the years with the Mayo News, founded in 1892, which has managed to keep going ever since. Someone else I knew well who was long based in Westport was a most charming specialist in repairing antique clocks, Jonathan Beech, a delightful person to know in the days when I covered the antiques trade, but he subsequently moved to Swinford in the same county.

Wexford

Over the years, I've made many trips to Wexford and enjoyed walks along the old timber quays and around its central streets, most historic and full of atmosphere. One firm I had many dealings with was Kelly's Bakery, which for years, operated from a lovely old fashioned shop on the Main Street, but is now in a modern factory on the outskirts of the town. In Wexford itself, I've enjoyed exploring old ruins like Selskar Abbey. A great friend of mine for many years in the journalism business was a Wexford native, Richard Roche, while Wexford has also produced one of Ireland's great contemporary literar figures, John Banville, the novelist, born there in 1945. Another Wexford person with whom Bernadette was once very friendly was Brendan Corish (1918-1990), a former leader of the Irish Labour Party.

Just 15 km south of Wexford, on the main road to Rosslare, there used to be another delightful spot to visit, the Yola Farmstead, with plenty of thatched cottages, all designed to commemorate the Yola tradition, a language unique to south Wexford, with Anglo-Norman origins, that managed to last until the 19th century. But sadly, the Yola Homestead is no more.

Wicklow Town

We've long been going to Wicklow town, where in the old days, we much enjoyed meals at the Grand Hotel as well as walks along the two piers in the town harbour, close to the port area. It's a very picturesque town, very historical, too. Robert Halpin, who became the skipper famous for his cable laying exploits, was born in the Bridge Inn, at the corner of the road leading down to the main pier, in 1836. He died in 1894, at his home, which is now Tinakilly Country House Hotel, from gangrene, after he had accidentally cut his foot while paring his toenails. He is also commemorated by a fine memorial in the Main Street.

Apart from the area around the harbour, where the River Vartry runs into the harbour is very scenic looking and there's a nearby attraction in the 18th century Church of Ireland church, with its Russian style copper copula. The other main church in the town is St Patrick's, the Catholic church, perched up on a hill. Wicklow is also noted for its old goal, now converted into a fine museum;it's reputed to be haunted. On its seaward side, Wicklow also has the ruins of the Black

Castle, which date from the 12th century. The centre of the town has changed comparatively little, but in recent decades, the town has been much expanded, with many houses built on the hillsides at the back of the town.

In more recent times, my main purpose in going to Wicklow town was to see Nell Kane, a wonderful music teacher, who was born in Wicklow town but whose family moved to Dublin when she was three. For many years in the 1950s and the 1960s, she ran her own orchestra, the Nell Kane Orchestra, which did many concerts for charity. Nell taught for years in the old college of music on Chatham Row in central Dublin, now part of the Dublin Institute of Technology. She spent the best part of 50 years teaching there and she didn't give up private teaching until she was 86. After she retired from the music college, she returned to her native Wicklow town and the old family home, Hillside Cottage, where she lived for the last 30 years of her life. Nell was marvellous company, totally au fait with everything that was going on right up to the end of her life, and I had many most enjoyable afternoons in her company, sometimes meeting the wonderful carers who looked after her. She died in St Vincent's Hospital, Dublin, at the end of March, 2016, having reached her 98th birthday in January, 2016. In September, 2016, I was privileged to meet many of her relatives at a lovely lunch in Tinakilly Country House Hotel.

Youghal

Youghal is a most appealing town, with an amazing variety of 18th century architecture, as well as even earlier buildings. In the late 16th century, Sir Walter Raleigh was mayor of Youghal and lived at Myrtle Grove, a fine old house that's still there. It's said that in 1585 he introduced potatoes to Ireland by planting them in the gardens of Myrtle Grove, while he also introduced tobacco to Ireland. Behind Myrtle Grove are the extensive medieval town walls, well preserved and every bit as impressive as the old city walls in Derry, although much less widely known.

Along the main street of Youghal are many fine 18th century houses, such as the Red House, while at one end of the main street is the clock gate tower. During the 1798 rebellion, many local rebels were hanged from it. These days, it has an altogether more peaceful purpose as a recently opened museum. Youghal also came to fame in the summer of 1954, when the waterfront of Youghal doubled as a New England whaling town, for the shooting of the Moby Dick film, starring Gregory Peck. Today, the Moby Dick Inn, near the harbour, still has many examples of memorabilia from that filming, as well as some star studded visitors' books. The area around the harbour is still very picturesque and if you walk out of town, towards the sea, you'll see the old lighthouse and Perks' amusement centre. When I was working on the Michelin Guide to Ireland, we stayed at the Devonshire Arms Hotel, often rather chilly, but replete with historical atmosphere. The place was built around 1780. The many historical intricacies of Youghal live on, making it one of the most fascinating towns in Ireland.

ends